GF891.A54 1997
Alexander, Bryan
The vanishing Arctic

P80717

South Puget Sound Community College

LIBRARY-MEDIA CENTER
SOUTH PUGET SOUND COMM. COLLEGE
2011 MOTTMAN RD SW
OLYMPIA, WA 98512-6292

P9-CJR-258

THE
VANISHING
ARCTIC

THE VANISHING ARCTIC

Bryan & Cherry Alexander

Facts On File, Inc.

LIBRARY-MEDIA CENTER
SOUTH PUGET SOUND COMM. COLLEGE
2011 MOTTMAN RD SW
OLYMPIA, WA 98512-6292

For Max and Andie

First published in 1996 in the United Kingdom by Blandford
an imprint of Cassell
CASSELL PLC
Wellington House
125 Strand
London WC2R 0BB

Text copyright © 1996 Bryan Alexander
Photographs copyright © 1996 Bryan & Cherry Alexander

The right of Bryan Alexander to be identified as author of this work has been asserted by him in accordance with the provisions of the UK Copyright, Designs and Patents Act 1988
First published in the United States by **Facts On File**, Inc. © 1997. All rights reserved. No part of this book may be reproduced or transmitted in any form or by any means, electronic or mechanical, including photocopying, recording or any information storage and retrieval system, without permission in writing from the copyright holder and publisher. For information contact: Facts On File, Inc. 11 Penn Plaza, New York, NY 10001. Facts On File books are available at special discounts when purchased in bulk quantities for businesses, associations, institutions or sales promotions. Please call our Special Sales Department in New York at 212/967-8800 or 800/322-8755.

Library of Congress Cataloging-in-Publication Data is available from
Facts On File, Inc.
ISBN 0-8160-3650-0
Map artwork Eugene Fleury
Design by Isobel Gillan
Printed and bound in Hong Kong by Dah Hua Ptg Ltd.

PAGE 1 *A Nenet boy proudly displays a fish caught in one of the lakes on the Yamal Peninsula, western Siberia.*
PAGES 2–3 *Autumn sunset near Savissivik, northern Greenland.*
INSET *With his harpoon at the ready an Inuk waits at a seal's breathing hole.*

Contents

PACIFIC OCEAN

•Anchorage

ALASKA

•Vancouver

CANADA

Churchill•

HUDSON BAY

Igloolik
Island

Hall Beach•

Ellesmere Island

Pond Inlet

FOXE BASIN

•Thule

JAMES BAY

•Savissivik

Baffin
Island

BAFFIN BAY

Lake
Bourinot

•Iqaluit

Mistassini•

GREENLAND

•Montreal

Nuuk•

Arctic Circle

ICELAND

ATLANTIC OCEAN

Preface

My interest in the Arctic began many years ago while I was studying photography in London. I visited the library at the Scott Polar Research Institute in Cambridge to read up on the technical problems of photography at sub-zero temperatures for a project I was working on. I soon became fascinated by the Arctic and particularly its native people. By the time I returned from my first trip to Greenland in 1971, where I spent several months living among the Inuit, I was well and truly hooked.

What I have always admired about the native peoples of the North is not just their ability to survive in such a difficult environment but also how they manage to live in harmony with it. They love their land, and few of the North's native people that I have met have ever expressed any interest in living elsewhere.

The cultures of most of the native peoples of the Arctic and Sub-Arctic are currently undergoing a period of great change. As the influences of the modern world are increasingly felt throughout the North, many of the traditional ways of its peoples have already disappeared forever; others will doubtless follow in the years ahead.

This book is not meant to be an anthropological guide. Its aim is to give a more intimate account of five distinct northern cultures. Through a combination of photographs and text, I hope to give the reader a feeling for this remarkable area of the world, as well as an insight into what life is like for some of the North's more traditional native people.

Each of the chapters in this book focuses on individual families from five different native groups that I have had the privilege to live and work among during the past decade.

ABOVE *The Greenland icecap near Cape York.*

LEFT *A polar bear by the ice edge, Spitsbergen.*

The Arctic
Great Northern Wilderness

ABOVE *After freeze-up in the autumn, a polar bear roams the newly formed ice of Hudson Bay in search of seals.*

LEFT *An aerial view of a pod of belugas swimming in peaty water at the mouth of Seal River in Hudson Bay. During the summer months, belugas often congregate in large numbers there.*

OVERLEAF *Gilded by late-afternoon sunshine, a large iceberg at the mouth of Wolstenholme Fjord in Northwest Greenland takes on the appearance of a giant meringue.*

ABOVE *Arctic avens (*Dryas integrifolia*) on summer tundra. The flowers act as a solar panel following the sun on its course round the sky.*

LEFT *Wind clouds forming over the tundra on Ellesmere Island, where cotton grass (*Eriophorum angustifolium*) thrives on boggy ground.*

BELOW *Surrounded by purple saxifrage (*Saxifraga oppositifolia*), a female eider duck (*Somateria mollissima*) incubates her eggs, well camouflaged on the summer tundra. Eholmen Island, Spitsbergen.*

LEFT *Arctic hares (*Lepus arcticus*) foraging under the midnight sun. Here on Ellesmere Island, Canada, they sometimes form groups of 1,000 or more.*

RIGHT *A pack of polar wolves (*Canis lupus*) roams the tundra of Ellesmere Island, Canada, in search of food. They feed mainly on Peary caribou and musk ox. A polar wolf needs several hundred square kilometres of hunting territory.*

BELOW *Musk oxen (*Ovibos moschatus*) galloping across the snow-covered tundra on Victoria Island, Canada. Their thick winter coats make them oblivious to the severe cold of the high Arctic.*

80717

17

SOUTH PUGET SOUND LIBRARY

ABOVE *A harp seal (*Phoca groenlandica*) surfaces among broken sea-ice. Each spring, many thousands of these seals breed on the ice-floes in the Gulf of St Lawrence, Canada.*

RIGHT *On the edge of an ice-floe off the coast of North Greenland, eider ducks (*Somateria mollissima*) bask in the midnight sun.*

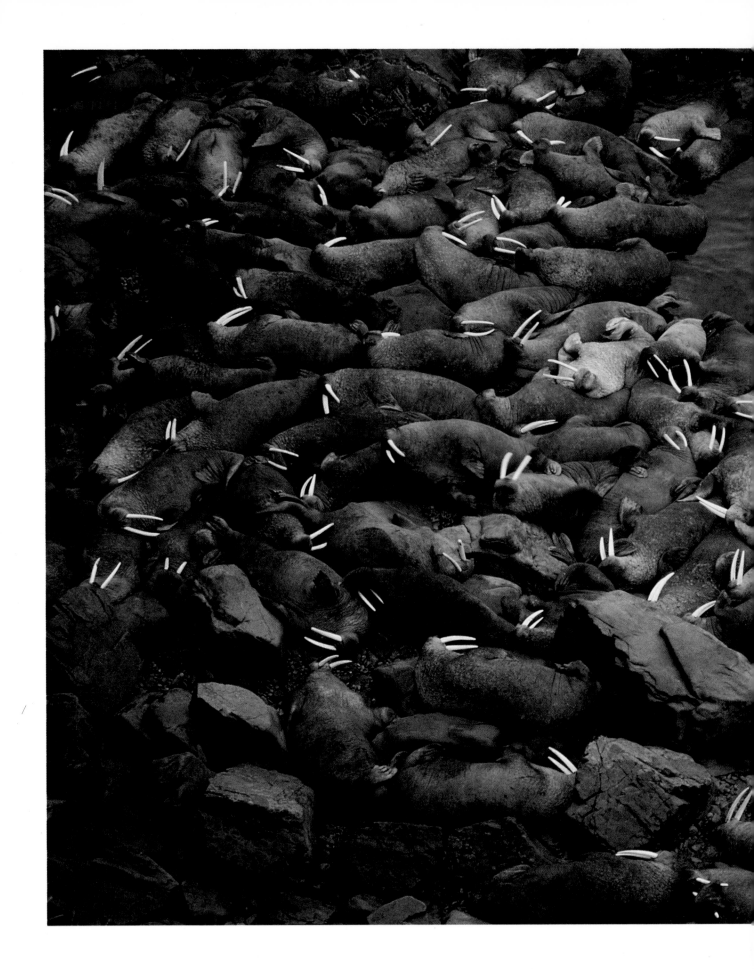

ABOVE AND LEFT *Pacific walrus (*Odobenus rosmarus divergens*) at a summer haul out on Round Island, Alaska. They spend most of the year on ice-floes, feeding on clams and other molluscs in shallow waters of the Arctic.*

OVERLEAF *A herd of caribou (*Rangifer tarandus*) crossing a tundra pond close to the coast of Hudson Bay. Mosquitos plague caribou during the summer and the animals will keep moving to avoid them.*

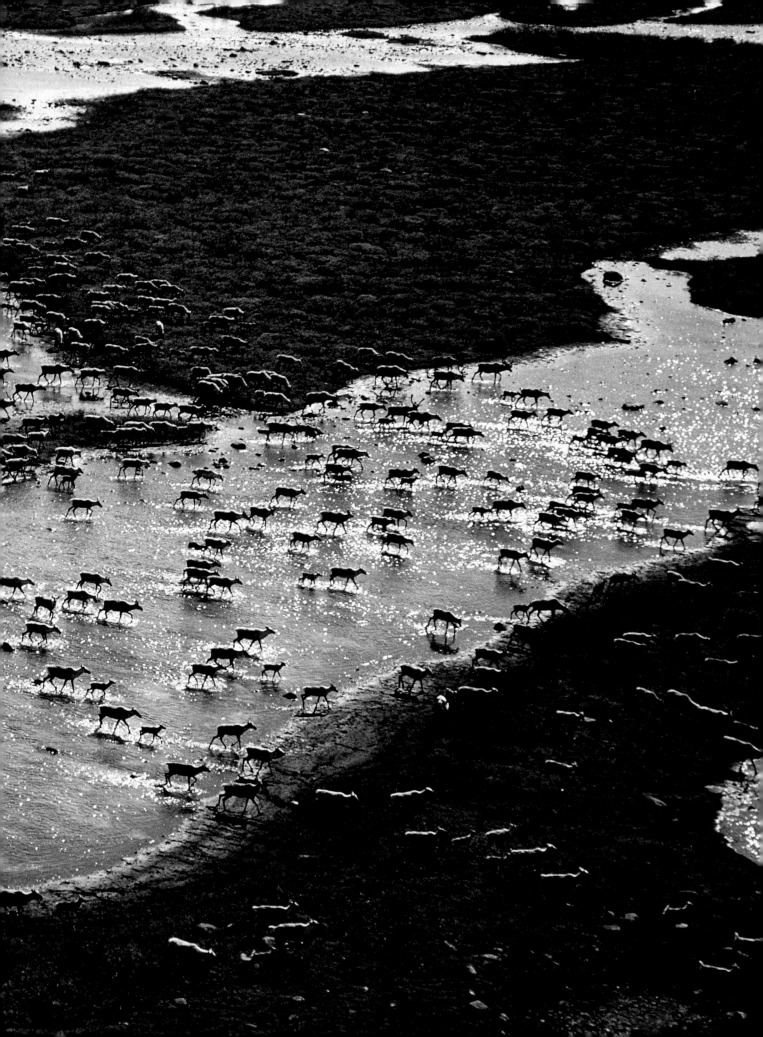

ABOVE AND LEFT *The Northern Lights (Aurora Borealis). These hanging curtains of the rippling light are a common sight on clear nights in the Arctic. The colour is usually pale green and sometimes deep red or violet.*

OVERLEAF *At noon on a January day in North Greenland, the full moon reflects off the surface of an iceberg polished by wind-driven particles of snow and ice.*

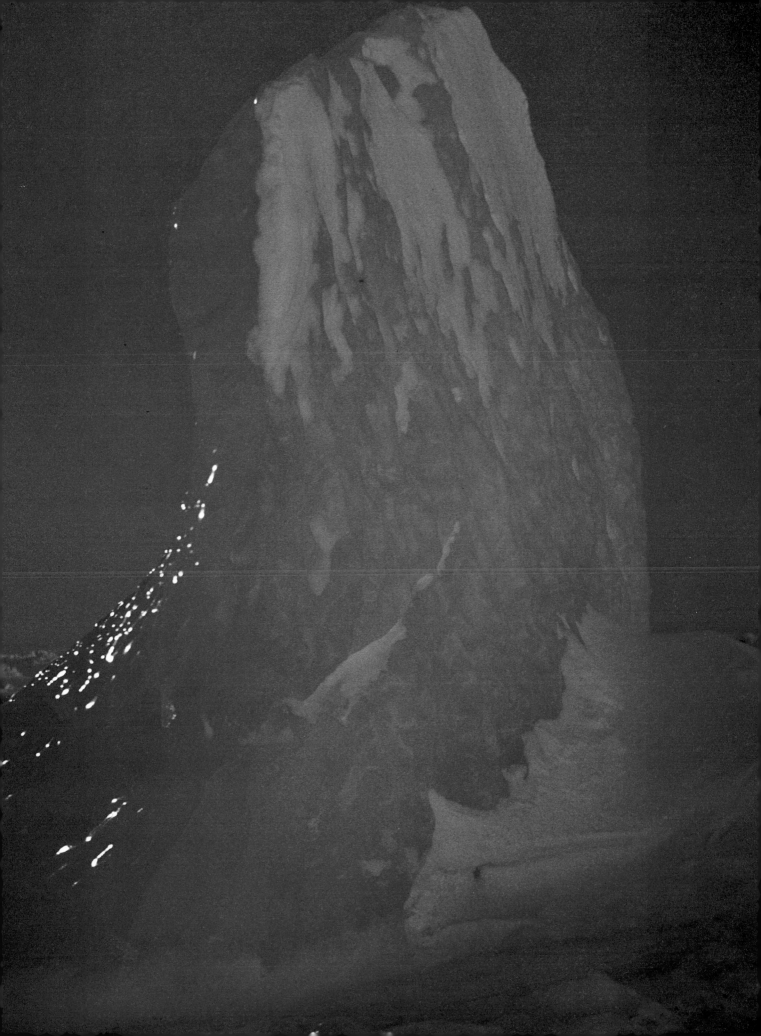

The Inuit of Northwest Greenland
The Hunt for Nanuq

The Inuit of the remote Avanersuaq region of Northwest Greenland are the most northerly indigenous people on Earth. Avanersuaq appropriately means 'the place of the farthest North'. Over the centuries the people of Avanersuaq have been known by a number of different names. The Scottish explorer John Ross, who, on his 'Voyage of Discovery' in 1818 was the first European to encounter these people, called them 'Arctic Highlanders'. Their Greenlandic neighbours to the south named them the Avanersuaqmiut ('people of the farthest North'). They have also been called 'Wild Gentlemen', 'Thule Eskimos' and 'Polar Eskimos'. In this book I have referred to them as the Inughuit (singular Inughuaq) which is the name they call themselves. It means 'great human beings'. The Inughuit speak a dialect of Greenlandic which has its roots in 'Inuktitut', the language spoken by the Inuit of northern Canada.

Avanersuaq has the harsh climate that is common to the high Arctic. Temperatures plunge to -40°F (-40°C) in winter and seldom get above 54°F (12°C) in July. During the summer the glaciers, which flow gradually from the inland icecap, calve countless icebergs into the coastal waters. For nine months of each year the surrounding seas remain frozen, giving the Inughuit an enormous range for travel by dogsled.

ABOVE *Sofie Jensen warmly wrapped up against the cold in a fox-fur hood.*

LEFT *To quench his thirst, a hunter drinks from a pool of meltwater on an iceberg.*

The Avanersuaq district lies between 75° and 80° North, stretching from Smith Sound in the north to Melville Bay in the south. At these latitudes the sun sets each October and doesn't appear above the horizon until the following February. Nature compensates for these months of darkness with a corresponding four-month period when the sun doesn't set.

There is archaeological evidence to suggest that the earliest settlers arrived in Avanersuaq some 5,000 years ago after crossing Smith Sound from Canada. The direct ancestors of today's Inughuit, however, belonged to the Thule culture and reached Avanersuaq soon after AD 1000.

Apart from seasonal visits by whalers in the nineteenth century, the Inughuit had relatively little contact with white people until the American explorer Robert Edwin Peary arrived in 1891. His association with them spanned 20 years as he made his repeated attempts to reach the North Pole. Like many early explorers he realized the value of having Inuit on Arctic expeditions and exploited their knowledge and skills. This ensured their lives would never be the same again.

Peary was followed by the Danish explorers Knud Rasmussen and Peter Freuchen. They too mounted Arctic expeditions from Avanersuaq and colonized the region for Denmark.

Today, there are approximately 1,000 Inughuit living in Avanersuaq. Around 700 live in the main settlement of Qaanaaq on the north side of Inglefield Sound. The remainder are scattered through the district's five other small villages.

Avanersuaq is one of the most traditional Inuit communities in the Arctic today. Hunting continues to be the main occupation, and traditional forms of transport like the dogsled and kayak are still in common use.

. . . .

It was a late February afternoon and already dark as I made my way across the village of Moriussaq to visit Ituko. The year's first sunshine, ending the four months of polar night, had only reached this part of North Greenland a week earlier, and the days were still very short. It was cold with a strong easterly wind and the hard-packed snow squeaked under my feet. The village seemed empty, a soft glow of light from the windows of some of the houses being the only sign of life. Moriussaq, which is home to about 60 Inughuit, lies on a narrow coastal plain. Behind it, steep hills rise up to the icecap, which stretches 700 miles to Greenland's east coast.

Ituko's hut was at the southern end of the village. His team of huskies lay curled motionless nearby, their backs to the wind and their noses tucked up under their tails as the blown snow drifted over them. I scrambled through the low porch and opened the door of the hut, relieved to be out of the biting wind. It was snug inside, and the interior of the hut was bathed in soft light from a kerosene lamp. Ituko and his

Avortuniaq outside her home in the village of Qaanaaq.

girlfriend Panerak both gave me welcoming smiles. She was nursing their two-month-old son, while Ituko was kneeling on the floor, surrounded by tools and wood shavings, measuring a long plank of wood. He brushed sawdust off his trousers as he stood up to greet me.

'I am making a new sled for the hunt,' Ituko explained. 'The box for the primus stove and kerosene will go here . . .', he traced an imaginary line across one of the planks. 'You'll sit there, me here, and there,' he said, tracing the final line, '. . . three polar bears!' It was a good joke and we all laughed. I had travelled with Ituko before on a bear hunt, and we had caught one bear in a month. Last year, he had drawn a blank. Three would be like winning the lottery.

Hunting polar bear on the sea-ice of Melville Bay is no easy task at the best of times. The weather can be fierce, the ice difficult to cross and there is the constant threat that the sea-ice may break up around those who venture onto it. These difficulties only add to the prestige of the few skilled hunters who do set out each winter in search of what the Inughuit have always considered to be the ultimate quarry. In the Avanersuaq district, polar bear is considered a delicacy. Some elderly Inuit, who have tried both, liken its taste to human flesh. But it is the skin that is the most highly prized part of a bear. Though their market value can be around US $1,500–2,000, few polar-bear skins from Avanersuaq end up decorating the houses of the wealthy; instead the Inughuit make warm durable trousers out of them as they have for centuries.

Ituko's home village of Moriussaq during the polar night.

At his home in Moriussaq, Ituko holds his son Igaja while Panerak softens a kamik *sole.*

I took off my Parka and mitts and warmed my hands over the oil stove before sitting down. Close to the stove, a shoulder of walrus meat, next day's dog food, hung from the ceiling to thaw. Panerak poured me some tea, while Ituko lit a primus stove and put a pan of seal meat on it to cook. Ituko checked his watch and then walked over to turn on his radio, as it was time for the evening news and weather. The forecast was not good for Thule – -20°F (-29°C) with winds up to 70 miles an hour. Persistent bad weather and ice conditions had meant that Ituko had not been able to go hunting for almost a month, and the whole village was short of meat. Ituko was a natural hunter, a man who couldn't stand to have a roof over his head during fine weather. This prolonged period of bad weather did have its up-side, as it had given him the opportunity to spend more time with his pride and joy, his newborn son Igaja.

Despite the recent bad weather, Ituko was in a buoyant mood and talked excitedly about preparations for the bear hunt: Panerak was making him a new pair of *kamik* (sealskin boots); the dog harnesses were repaired; 22 gallons of kerosene should be enough; and he was considering bringing along Jens, another skilled hunter who wanted to come with us.

The smell of the cooking seal meat gradually filled the hut until Ituko removed the saucepan from the primus stove. He scooped out the chunks of seal meat, placing them on a tray in the middle of the floor. We sat round the tray and took it in turns to skewer

Ituko trains his dogs to harass polar bears by imitating a bear and its behaviour.

one of the chunks of meat with a knife, holding it in the air to cool off before we ate it. Seal meat is tender, dark, rather oily, and has always been the staple of the Inughuit diet.

After I had finished, Ituko pointed over towards a large sink with chrome taps, and I went over to wash my hands. Ituko had got the sink from the garbage dump near the American airbase at Thule. I remembered how on the first occasion after I had eaten at Ituko's home I had walked over to the sink and instinctively turned one of the taps. Ituko had roared with laughter because Moriussaq, like most of the local Inughuit villages, has no running water. The Inughuit have to collect glacial ice to melt for water. He later confided to me that he derived great amusement from watching European visitors attempting to get water out of his taps.

We were sitting drinking more tea after the meal when we heard footsteps outside. Moments later, Ituko's brother, Tukak, entered. He was one of a succession of Inughuit who visited that evening. As they entered, each was heralded by a cloud of cold air that drifted across the floor of the hut like dry ice across a theatre stage. Some only stayed a few minutes; others stopped for an hour or more drinking tea and engaging in relaxed conversation. Visiting has always been an important part of the social life of the Inughuit. It's the main way that the latest news, gossip and scandal spreads through the communities, and is often referred to as the 'Kamik Telegraph'.

Two weeks later, Ituko had transformed four planks of wood into a finished sled. A period of cold and stable weather had developed. It was time, Ituko reckoned, for us to leave. On 14 March we went to the small store in Moriussaq to buy supplies. The shop was typical of those in North Greenland's small communities where supplies come once a year by ship. They carry limited stock – just the basics for a hunter's life in the Arctic and enough sweets, potato chips and fizzy drinks to keep today's Inughuit children happy.

We bought kerosene, rope, ammunition, tobacco, tea, sugar, packet soups, oats, margarine and 25 packets of ship's biscuits. These biscuits are about 3 inches square and rock hard, and have been the staple carbohydrate of Greenland's hunters for many years and are made by a Danish dog biscuit manufacturer.

By mid-afternoon, all our hunting equipment and supplies were securely lashed to the two sleds and we were ready to leave. Ituko and Jens hitched up their dogs and, after waving farewell to family and friends, led them out of the village and down onto the sea-ice. The dogs' excitement was at fever pitch, with the two teams racing each other as we set off across the frozen sea. After a while their initial burst of energy waned and the dogs settled down to a steady trot.

Once clear of the village we entered the silent world of the high Arctic in winter. The swish of the sled runners on the hard-packed snow, the panting of the dogs and Ituko's and Jens' occasional shouts of encouragement to their teams were the only sounds as we travelled across the sea-ice.

Snow-covered huskies. The snow insulates them against the wind and cold.

We headed southeast, following the coast towards Wolstenholme Fjord. Our plan was to pick up some walrus meat that Ituko had cached at Uummannaq (Dundas) the previous spring. With 27 large huskies and ourselves to feed, we needed a lot of meat. The weather was perfect, with not a breath of wind, and the afternoon winter sunshine bathed the sea-ice in a soft golden light. Our route took us close to Manson Island where hundreds of eider ducks breed each summer; now locked by snow and ice, this flat island seemed lifeless except for a lone raven that took to the air to follow us for a while.

LEFT *Ituko lights two primus stoves to heat his tent while camped out on the ice of Melville Bay.*

OPPOSITE *Ituko frosted up while out hunting. The temperature was -22°F (-30°C).*

We reached Uummannaq at sunset, and Ituko and Jens led their dogs through the tidal ice and up onto the beach to a pile of rocks where the meat was cached. Taking their ice-chisels and a shovel from the sleds, Ituko and Jens dug away some of the snow and then began to move the rocks. It was then we encountered our first setback of the trip. A combination of the spray from autumn storms and a brief thaw in December had resulted in the large pieces of meat becoming frozen together and encased in ice. We had a 2-ton block of frozen walrus meat to deal with, and recovering it was going to be a slow process.

They decided that we should spend the night here and we prepared to make camp. The dogs were unhitched and tethered close by. Both sleds were emptied and put side by side and a tent erected over them. Caribou skins were spread out over the sleds for us to sleep on, and once the two primus stoves had been lit it was soon warm inside. We brewed tea, and afterwards returned to the task of recovering the walrus meat. Ituko and Jens set about the frozen meat with a pickaxe and an ice-chisel.

It was a magical night. As darkness fell, Uummannaq's distinctive tabletop mountain looked spectacular in the moonlight, while the lights of Thule airbase flickered in the distance. Close to the beach were the remains of some old houses. Uummannaq, as the Inughuit called this place, was once the hub of polar Eskimo society. It was here that the famous Danish explorers Knud Rasmussen and Peter Freuchen established the district's first trading post in 1910. They gave it the name 'Thule' after the latin *ultima Thule* ('faraway unknown region'), and it was from here that they set out on their famous Thule expeditions.

The Inughuit community at Uummannaq became an early casualty of the Cold War. In 1951 construction began on the building of a US airbase at Pituffik ('the place where dogs are tied up'), only a few miles from Uummannaq. Two years later, the 100 or so Inughuit (27 families) who lived at Uummannaq were 'persuaded' or, some believe, forced to abandon their homes and hunting-grounds and move 62 miles north to Qaanaaq. Today, a few buildings, empty missile silos and a commemorative stone to Knud Rasmussen are all that is left at Uummannaq.

It was midnight before Ituko and Jens had finished extracting as much meat as we needed from the frozen ground. Afterwards they chopped some of the meat into small pieces with a hatchet and fed their dogs. Walrus meat is considered by the

Ituko feeds seal meat to his dog-team. He throws the meat to each dog in turn.

Inughuit to be the best and most sustaining dog food, and now we had enough to feed the teams for several days. We would also eat walrus that night. Ituko brought a large chunk back to the tent and we cut pieces off and ate them raw. It was tender, but tasted bitter, which was not surprising considering it was nine months old. I ate a few pieces as quickly as possible, for I knew that once the meat thawed in the warmth of the tent its pungent smell would make me retch if I attempted to eat it.

Most Inughuit enjoy eating decaying meat. They relish a local delicacy called *kiviat* which is made by fermenting little auks inside a sealskin. I, like many Europeans, find decomposed meat difficult to eat. On the other hand, Ituko disliked strong cheese. One time when I had been living with him and his family I had bought some mature and rather smelly Danish cheese at Thule airbase. After a while the smell of the cheese got to Ituko and he took it outside and placed it on the roof of his hut, muttering something about it smelling like old *kamik* (sealskin boots).

Travelling on hunting trips with Ituko was always enjoyable but never comfortable. He was usually too busy hunting to carry out more than cursory maintenance and repairs to his equipment. His boats and his tents always leaked. As I climbed into my sleeping-bag that night I realized that this trip would be no different. It was about -22°F (-30°C), and through a hole in the roof of the tent above my head I could see the stars.

The next morning, after a breakfast of tea and ship's biscuits, we began the task of breaking camp and re-packing the sleds. To me the weather seemed perfect – calm, cold and sunny with barely a cloud in the sky. Jens thought otherwise. He pointed to a thin strip of cloud above Pingarssuit mountain and told me he thought that there would be a storm later. Apart from a slight breeze that gently flapped the tent walls, there was no sign of any wind, but I had learnt from previous experience not to question the Inughuit judgement on weather.

It was nearly midday before everything was securely lashed down on the sleds and we were ready to move. Ituko led the way, while I travelled behind with Jens. Once down on the sea-ice, the dogs set off at a steady trot around the base of Uummannaq's mountain. The US Airforce officers had found their own use for this tabletop mountain: each summer they hold a golf tournament on top of it.

As we approached the south side of the mountain, Jens' weather prediction began to materialize. The easterly breeze strengthened, blowing snow that snaked across the surface of the sea-ice. As the wind developed into a storm, our visibility gradually deteriorated. First we lost sight of Ituko's sled some 30 yards in front of us; then our own dogs began to disappear from view. Jens and I sat on the sled with our backs to the wind, our heads bowed as the blown snow swirled around us. I have never ceased to be amazed by the ability of the Inuit to navigate in such conditions. Every so often, Jens would shout a command to the dogs or use his whip as they trotted slowly and reluctantly across North Star Bay. We were making slow progress.

Once, as I glanced behind me, I saw a dark shape which appeared to be moving in our direction. It was difficult to make out what it was through the blowing snow.

ABOVE *As the winter sun sets, Panigpak prepares to harpoon a seal at its breathing-hole.*

LEFT *Ituko catches little auks near Narssaarssuk, with the aid of an* ipu *(long-handled net).*

Only when it was close did I realize that the object was a 40-gallon oildrum, rolling and tumbling across the ice, propelled by the fierce wind.

Jens turned round towards me. 'We are going to Narssaarssuk; there are houses there,' he yelled, trying to make himself heard above the wind. The thought of a hut we could shelter in was most appealing. I was already feeling chilled and certainly not relishing the idea of a long day's travel in this storm.

Narssaarssuk is a hunting-camp situated on a flat coastal plain on the south side of Bylot Sound. It doesn't look much – about eight small shacks built by the Inughuit themselves, largely from materials scavenged from the airbase. Narssaarssuk is a good place from which to hunt seal and walrus during the winter months, and Inughuit from Moriussaq and some of the district's other communities usually move there each autumn after freeze-up.

A couple of hours later, we were stopped by a wall of ice. We had reached Narssaarssuk at low tide and the land was nearly 6 feet above us. Jens led the dogs through the tidal ice until he found a suitable place for the dogs to scramble up onto land, while I guided the sled with the upstanders. The wind was still blowing hard and only a couple of the huts were visible through the blowing snow. Ituko had arrived a few minutes ahead of us and had just finished tethering his dogs. He was in the process of digging away snow that had drifted against the door of the hut we would use.

The hut, Ituko told me, belonged to a hunter from Moriussaq. It was tiny, almost half of the interior being taken up by a wooden sleeping platform. But its size made it easy to heat and within 15 minutes of lighting a primus stove it was pleasantly warm inside. We gradually thawed out, helped by some hot tea. Then we did what all Inughuit do when they first arrive in a community – we went visiting.

Our first stop was Jess Qujaukitsok's hut. As we approached, Ituko paused and said to me, jokingly, 'The King of Narssaarssuk's house'. Jess was the oldest hunter at Narssaarssuk and had spent many winters here. The hut was warm inside and filled with the smell of cooking seal meat. Jess was seated on the sleeping platform smoking a pipe while his wife, Isigaitsoq, was seated on a stool, busy scraping the fat off a sealskin with an *ulu* (woman's knife). She broke off from her work to make us tea and serve us some freshly cooked seal meat. The men exchanged news and talked of hunting. It had not been good recently but Jess had caught two seals the previous day in nets set under the ice. For a man approaching 70 he was remarkably spry, with a thick mop of hair. He still ran a dog-team and hunted regularly out of Narssaarssuk, helped by Thomas, one of his grandsons.

After leaving Jess, we went on to visit Karkutsiaq, a young hunter from Moriussaq, together with his wife Tabitha. We drank more tea and ate *quaq* (frozen raw meat) from a large chunk of whale meat placed on a plastic sheet in the middle of the floor. Their hut was tiny, no more than 4 x 3 yards. On a shelf by the small window, Karkutsiaq's radio was tuned into the airbase, and a DJ was playing country-and-western music. Every so often the programme was interrupted by a weather warning. The temperature was -20°F (-29°C) and winds were out of the east gusting up to 70 miles per hour.

Winter storms in which ferocious katabatic winds blow off the icecap are not uncommon in this part of Greenland; winds of up to 203 miles per hour have been recorded at Thule airbase.

The American military like to have their home comforts when they are stationed abroad. Despite Thule's isolated and remote location, only 800 miles from the North Pole, it is remarkably well equipped with leisure facilities. It has a theatre, bowling alley, gymnasium and cocktail bars, as well as restaurants where diners can eat high-quality Danish and American food.

Although in Karkutsiaq's hut at Narssaarssuk we were only about 11 miles from the airbase, we were a world apart from life there. As the evening progressed, several other Inughuit joined us in the hut until there was barely room to move. The atmosphere was light-hearted. Ituko was on form, laughing and joking as we played cards into the early hours of the morning by the light of a kerosene lamp.

We awoke the next morning to discover that the storm had blown itself out in the night and we had perfect weather again. We packed the sleds and set off with Ituko leading the way as we headed east along the coast. Ituko was worried that yesterday's storm would have blown the ice out from around Quarautit (Cape Atholl) and we would not be able to get round. His fears were unfounded. When we reached the Cape, the ice was good, and, after rounding it, we began to head south towards Ivnaanganeq (Cape York). Our plan was to head for the ice of Melville Bay where polar bears are often found roaming during the winter months. There was however a down-side to this. Melville Bay is notorious for its treacherous pack-ice, which is often difficult to cross because of its high pressure ridges. Buffeted by high winds, the ice is constantly on the move, drifting between Greenland and Canada. It is usually only accessible to the Inughuit when a favourable wind has blown it against the landfast ice of the Greenland coast.

Dogsled travel might be slow, but in fine weather and with good ice conditions I have always enjoyed it. You have time to observe your surroundings and chat with your travelling companions. If you feel cold, you can always get off the sled and run alongside for a while until you warm up. As we slowly made our way along the rugged coastline, Ituko pointed out old Inughuit campsites. We talked about hunting and he told me how his father, Kavigarssuak, had travelled this route with Knud Rasmussen. His father was one of the Inughuit who accompanied Rasmussen on his epic 'Fifth Thule Expedition' from North Greenland, across Canada and Alaska to Siberia.

Ituko and Jens scanned the surrounding ice for seal breathing-holes, and about every three hours or so we stopped to untangle the dogs' traces and make some hot tea to warm us up. We were making good progress and by late afternoon we crossed the sea-ice at the mouth of the Pituffik glacier. There were several large icebergs nearby, locked in by the sea-ice for the winter.

A short while later we came across a long lead in the ice that ran parallel with the coast. We followed the edge of the lead in the hope that we would see some seals in the open water. Sure enough, just after sunset, a seal's head broke the calm surface of the

During the winter darktime, Ituko checks a seal's breathing-hole.

water in the lead; then it dived again almost immediately. Jens and Ituko quickly stopped their dogs. They each grabbed a rifle and harpoon and ran to the edge of the lead. They waited motionless for a while, and then the seal surfaced again, this time quite close to Jens. He raised his rifle and shot it and then managed to harpoon it before it could sink. It was a large bearded seal, about 8 feet long, and it took the three of us to haul it up onto the ice. Ituko and Jens were delighted as we now had fresh meat. They quickly set about butchering the carcass and dividing up the meat and skin between them. The thick, tough skin of the bearded seal is prized by the Inughuit for making boot soles as well as dog whips and rope.

Darkness was closing in, so once the butchering was complete and the meat loaded on the sled we set off in search of a safe place to spend the night. A short while later, we made camp on the sea-ice, close to the small island of Iganaq ('conical rock'). Ituko and Jens fed their dogs on the fresh seal meat. Later we boiled up some of the intestines for our evening meal and ate them with raw fat. The intestines were tasty but rather rubbery; all in all I thought the dogs had got the better meal, but I had to admit they had worked for it.

I was woken the following morning by the sound of the tent walls flapping in a strong breeze. It had clouded over and it was much warmer. The wind was blowing from the west, the right direction for us as it would move the drifting ice towards the Greenland coast. After breaking camp, we headed towards the island where we clambered over ridges of tidal ice and up onto the land. From a steep snow-covered slope on the west side of the island, Ituko and Jens scanned the surrounding sea through binoculars. There was no sign of polar bears, but there was ice to the west of us for as far as the eye could see. Ituko thought we might be able to get out onto the pack-ice from near Iganaq; so, after getting back down onto the sea-ice, we set off heading west across the frozen sea.

Soon, however, we encountered a wide area of new ice. We tried to cross it, but it was so thin that it bowed under the weight of our dogs and sleds, forcing us to turn back to firm ice and head south again. In the afternoon we tried again to head west across some rough pressure-ice. After some gruelling sledging that entailed getting ourselves, the dogs and sleds over 6-foot-high ridges of pressure-ice, we were forced once again to turn back when a large expanse of open water barred our way. The only encouraging thing was that we came across several sets of polar-bear tracks. They were all old, but old bear tracks were better than no bear tracks.

By dusk, we were all tired and made camp close to an iceberg. While I boiled up some bearded seal meat for our evening meal, Jens and Ituko fed the dogs, dividing them into four groups and tethering them on all sides of the tent to give us warning should a curious bear decide to pay us a visit during the night. Jens also released one of his team so it could roam loose around the camp. 'Our police dog,' Jens said, with a laugh.

Jens aims his rifle at a seal that has surfaced in open water at the floe edge, Cape York.

The next morning the weather was bad again. The tent was flapping violently in a strong southerly wind. Blown snow snaked across the ice and the dogs lay curled up tightly with their backs to the wind. We had a leisurely breakfast of tea, porridge oats and ship's biscuits with jam, as we waited for the weather to improve. Ituko and Jens related their dreams from the previous night, something that they did most mornings. 'I dreamt that I was chasing a bear,' Jens said, 'but just as my dogs got close to it the bear turned into a raven and it flew away.' They would often ask me about my dreams and obviously found it odd that I was seldom able to remember them.

Around midday, the wind suddenly stopped as though someone had turned it off with a switch. Before breaking camp, Ituko boiled up some more bearded seal meat to set us up for the day. I used the opportunity to wander off to answer the call of nature. I was on my way back to the tent when a patch of hard snow I was crossing gave way under me, and before I knew it I was in water surrounded by slush. I yelled to the others for help but with the primus stove roaring in the tent they didn't hear me. After a few seconds of flailing my arms in all directions I found some firm ice to my left, and after a brief struggle I managed to haul myself up onto it. I was only about 200 yards from our camp, and so I jogged back.

By the time I reached the tent, my outer clothing had frozen hard as a board. Falling through the ice is something that happens to most Inuit hunters from time to time. They take this kind of incident in their stride, and so I was determined not to make a big deal out of it. I entered the tent and in the calmest voice I could muster I announced what was plainly obvious – I had fallen through the ice. Ituko and Jens were visibly shocked and concerned. They quickly helped me out of my clothes and I crawled into my sleeping-bag while they made hot tea and hung my clothes up in the roof of the tent to dry. I felt bad, as I knew that they both wanted to be on the move and I was responsible for delaying our departure. While my clothes were drying, Ituko and Jens went to investigate the scene of the incident. When they returned they said I had been very lucky to get out. The ice all around was rotten and I had been very fortunate in finding the one spot where the ice was firm enough for me to be able to haul myself out.

By mid-afternoon my clothes were dry and we were able to pack the sleds and set off once again. That afternoon we were to experience the Arctic winter at its most beautiful. For much of the time we followed the edge of the ice along a large expanse of open water. Frost-smoke rising from the sea was turned gold by the late-afternoon sun. Two pairs of black guillemots in their striking winter plumage swam along the ice edge, their reflection mirrored in the calm water. Later, a bearded seal breached 6 feet clear of the water like a humpback whale. We passed several icebergs, including one that appeared like a castle in the mist.

Just before dusk, Jens shot a ringed seal that surfaced in the open water. It was quite far from the ice edge, so he used a small piece of ice as a raft, which he paddled with his harpoon, in order to retrieve it. Jens skinned and butchered the seal immediately. We ate the liver raw while it was still warm which gave us all a valuable dose of vitamin C. Raw seal liver has the same vitamin C content as grapefruit. We followed the liver with a hot meal of boiled ribs and heart. The rest of the seal was fed to the dogs. As darkness fell and we made camp for the night, the weather deteriorated again. The wind picked up and there was blowing snow. A halo round the moon that night, Ituko told me, was an indication that the sea-ice might break.

Over the coming days, our travel developed into a routine. We would set off mid-morning, always trying to head west. We would climb icebergs to check for any signs of polar bears and plan our best route across the sea-ice. Almost inevitably, high pressure ridges, thin ice or open water would end up barring our way and we would end up having to head south once again.

Jens uses an iceberg as a vantage point to scan the surrounding sea-ice for bears.

On 21 March I awoke to hear Ituko and Jens talking excitedly outside the tent. I put on my Parka and scrambled outside to find out what was happening. I was greeted by an alarming sight. We were adrift on an ice-floe surrounded by open sea. The ice around our camp had broken up during the night and we had not woken. We were about 15 miles from land, west of Ivnaanganeq (Cape York) and drifting slowly northeastwards on a floe, about 150 x 75 yards, that Ituko described as 'a little big'.

I suddenly had this overwhelming feeling of *déjà-vu*. Some years before I had been out walrus-hunting with three Inughuit in the north of the Avanersuaq district when the ice had broken up around us. Then we ended up adrift for three days before being rescued by helicopter. With little in the way of supplies, it had not been a pleasant experience, and certainly was not one I wanted to repeat.

For the moment there was nothing we could do but wait. After our usual breakfast, Ituko and Jens waited by the edge of the floe with their rifles and harpoons in case a seal surfaced nearby. We were desperately short of meat for our dogs. This was the first day of spring. It was cold with a bitter easterly wind, and here we were adrift on an ice-floe. The new season had certainly got off to an inauspicious start.

The hours passed slowly. Then in the late afternoon there was a change in the weather. The wind swung round and began to blow with increasingly strong gusts from the south. The sea became choppy and our ice-floe began to break up. Things were beginning to look dangerous. We were soon among a mass of loose ice that was being blown rapidly northwards. We quickly took down the tent, packed the sleds and hitched up the dogs so we were ready to move.

As the loose ice closed in around us, Ituko and Jens tried to figure a way across the floes towards the landfast ice. We began to move the dogs and sleds quickly, but carefully, from one floe to the next. It was not easy, as by now the floes were heaving in the heavy swell; to make matters worse, it was almost dark. Dogs and sleds fell in the water and were hauled out again. Jens' sled overturned completely and smashed an upstander. From all around us came the frightening sound of crunching ice as floes 2 feet thick smashed into each other.

After three hours of gruelling sledging, there was a yell of glee in the darkness from Ituko as we reached safe ice. The wind was blowing hard and it was bitterly cold; we stopped in the lee of an iceberg to untangle the dogs' traces and brew up some tea. Over a mug of hot tea we deliberated what to do next. We could either camp nearby or travel on to Ivnaanganeq (Cape York) and spend the night in one of the hunters' huts there. I was tired and relished the thought of a night in a warm hut. Ituko and Jens did not seem quite as enthusiastic as I was, for they knew that there would be hunters from Savissivik there.

Savissivik is the most southerly village in the Avanersuaq district. About half of the village's 120 inhabitants are Inughuit, while the other half are incomers, mainly from Kullorsuaq ('devil's thumb'), the most northerly community in the Upernavik

A hunter untangles the traces of his dog-team during a winter hunt.

district. Neither Ituko or Jens hid their feelings towards these Kullorsuarmiut. 'They have fleas,' Ituko told me. 'They even drink from the same mug!' Jens was quick to add. Drinking from someone else's mug has been frowned upon in Avanersuaq since the days when tuberculosis was rife.

Eventually the decision was made to go to Ivnaanganeq (Cape York), and, after we had finished drinking our tea and the dogs' traces had been untangled, Ituko led the way towards the cape while I travelled behind with Jens. Ten years Ituko's junior and more of an introvert, Jens was always good company to travel with. They were the two best hunters in Moriussaq and, although at times I sensed some competition between them, they often hunted together and made a good partnership.

LEFT Jens and Ituko enjoy a game of cards with Qitdlak Suersaq in a hunters' hut at Cape York.

OVERLEAF Kulutenguak out hunting in the ice-strewn waters of Inglefield Bredning.

After rounding the towering cliffs of Ivnaanganeq, Jens pointed to a dim light shining from a hut up on the hillside. There were several dog-teams tethered out on the ice, and they howled as we approached. After unhitching the sled and untangling the dogs' traces, Ituko and Jens secured their teams to the ice before we set off up the steep and icy hillside towards the light. There were three huts there. Ituko paused outside the largest and, before entering, he turned to me, grinning in the moonlight, and began to scratch imaginary flea-bites all over his body. Then we all quietly entered the hut. It was wonderfully warm inside, and a single kerosene lamp hanging from the ceiling threw a dim golden light across the platform where eight hunters lay sleeping. Two of them woke as we entered, and, with true Inuit hospitality, got up to prepare us hot tea and a meal of boiled seal meat. While we ate, Ituko and Jens recounted the events of the past few days. Then, after spreading our caribou skins over what little space remained on the sleeping platform, we lay down to rest.

The following morning I awoke to find that most of the others were already up sitting around chatting and smoking. The weather was bad and nobody would go hunting today. A strong wind was blowing from the east, which was bad news for us as it would blow the ice away from the Greenland coast towards Canada.

For most of the morning we lounged around the hut. Ituko and Jens repaired a few of their dogs' harnesses while they chatted with the other hunters. One of the Savissivik hunters gave us two seals so that Ituko and Jens could feed their dogs.

Later that night, it seemed as though everyone at Ivnaanganeq had crammed into our hut. Two saucepans of seal meat were put on primus stoves to cook. It turned into a boisterous evening. In the dim light and smoke-filled atmosphere the hunters joked and played cards into the early hours of the morning. It was in this kind of gathering that Ituko came into his element as the life and soul of the party.

The weather was greatly improved the next morning, but with the wind still blowing from the east there was no chance of us being able to get out onto the ice of Melville Bay. So Ituko and Jens decided to join the other hunters who were planning to return to Savissivik. We left at midday, in a convoy of sleds, weaving our way through a group of large icebergs that were frozen into the sea ice. Conditions were perfect for sledging; there was a covering of hard-packed snow on the ice, and the dogs trotted along at a steady pace.

It took about five hours to reach Savissivik, our journey only being interrupted by one brief tea stop. The spell of good weather was short-lived, as darkness fell, the wind swung round to the southwest and it became stormy again. By then, we were settled in the house of Ituko's friends Filoman and Mikissuk Karlsen. Our stay in Savissivik enabled us to get some more meat for our dogs and pick up some supplies from the village store, which was surprisingly well stocked for such a small and isolated community.

On the morning of 25 March the weather was cold, clear and calm. Ituko and Jens were keen to make an early start and we joined a stream of dogsleds leaving the village as hunters set out to make the most of the good weather. We headed southwest from Savissivik past Bushnan Island, close to where the Scottish explorer John Ross had first encountered the Inughuit in 1818.

Jens had a cousin in Savissivik, Jerimias Petersen, who followed us out onto the ice. The plan was to go seal-hunting first, as we still needed more meat for the dogs and ourselves, and then to try once again to get onto the drifting ice-sheets of Melville Bay. After an hour, a wide lead barred our way and we followed the edge of it until we saw a seal surface. Ituko stopped his dogs, and grabbed his rifle, but the seal dived before he could fire. When Jens and Jerimias caught up with Ituko they decided to spread out and wait to see if there were more seals nearby. They sat on their sleds about 100 yards apart and waited.

It was a beautiful day, and despite the cold it was pleasant to be out. We didn't have to wait long before a seal surfaced and Jerimias shot it. The seal was floating about 50 yards from the edge of the lead. Jerimias had brought along a kayak, which

A hunter rescues his dogs from the water after they had fallen through thin ice.

was lashed to his sled. After launching it from the edge of the ice, he paddled out through the curtain of ice-smoke which hung above the surface of the freezing water to retrieve the seal.

Later Jens also shot a seal, and once again Jerimias paddled his kayak out into the lead to retrieve it. It turned into a light-hearted day's hunting with a lot of banter. While we waited for more seals to appear, we ate raw seal liver with fat and washed it down with hot tea. Seals are curious creatures and the hunters tried a variety of sounds to lure them close. They tapped their sleds, scraped the ice with a harpoon and called out 'carrh, carrh, carrh'. These techniques seemed to prove effective on occasions, and by late afternoon Jerimias and Jens had shot two seals each.

Just before sunset we parted company with Jerimias. He was returning to Savissivik, but before leaving he gave us the two seals he had shot. For us they would be valuable dog food, and in return Jens gave him the skins from his two seals. Then we headed west to try once again to get out onto the ice of Melville Bay.

This time we had more luck. We crossed some sheets of newly formed ice that were so thin that on two occasions Ituko's sled broke through, but the dogs managed to haul us out. There was also a brief moment of excitement when a narwhal surfaced in a lead close by, sending up a cloud of exhaled breath into the cold air before it quickly dived again.

Once we reached pack-ice we encountered deep snow and high-pressure ridges which proved tricky to cross. Gradually the ice conditions improved as we headed further west. It was a bright night and the full moon reflecting off the ice and snow enabled us to travel until midnight.

The next day we had perfect weather again, and at midday we packed the sleds and set off again, still heading west away from the Greenland coast out into Melville Bay. Our search for polar bears had begun in earnest. Every three or four hours we stopped for a tea break, a chance to warm up and scan the surrounding ice for any sign of bears. We came across several sets of tracks, but on examining them they all proved to be old.

It was in the late afternoon that we came across two sets of bear tracks. Ituko and Jens quickly examined them. They were fresh! They were still soft and perhaps only an hour or so old. We followed the tracks for a couple of hours as they led us a difficult route across rough ice. Then from a high pressure ridge we briefly caught sight of the bears in the distance before they disappeared amongst the pressure ridges. Suddenly the whole atmosphere of the hunt changed. Ituko and Jens discussed strategy in a hurried whisper as we quickly unlashed the sleds, discarding anything that was not absolutely essential.

Jens with his dog-team sledging over pressure-ice near Cape York.

A polar bear can easily outpace a team of dogs pulling a sled over rough ice, so it was important that the sleds were as light as possible. We set off, with Ituko leading the way while I travelled behind with Jens. From then on, they communicated with gestures and imitated a raven's call to attract each other's attention. Ituko had once explained this by telling me that 'the raven and the polar bear are friends'. Ravens will scavenge from kill-sites of polar bears, so one can presume that polar bears are not alarmed by the familiar sound of a raven.

OPPOSITE A hunter checks polar-bear tracks on a piece of ice in Melville Bay.

RIGHT In a bid to escape the hunters and their dogs, a polar bear takes refuge in a lead.

The dogs seemed to sense the excitement, and with lighter loads we were able to travel much faster. However, it was not long before the bears became aware of us and separated. Ituko followed one set of tracks south, while Jens and I followed the other set west. After a while Jens shouted in dismay as the bear tracks we were following ended at a wide lead. Our bear had swum across a stretch of open water and given us the slip. We retraced our own tracks and then followed Ituko's. It was sunset when we caught sight of him in the distance, just as he was getting close to the bear. Running alongside the sled he kept shouting encouragement to his team. Then he used a snowknife to cut the traces of six of his best dogs. Free from the sled, they ran flat out after the bear. Suddenly the bear stopped and turned to face the six dogs, which quickly surrounded it, barking furiously. Ituko grabbed his rifle and fired, hitting the bear in the shoulder. In a last bid for freedom, the bear lunged forward, catching one of the dogs with a swipe of its forepaw. The dog howled in pain and retreated, while the bear headed for a nearby lead and plunged into the water. Ituko was quickly on the scene. He grabbed his harpoon and hurled it at the bear, hitting it in the chest and killing it instantly. It sank beneath the surface of the water.

Ituko hurls his harpoon at a polar bear in a lead.

Ituko and Jens hauled the bear to the surface with the harpoon line, and then with considerable effort dragged the animal up onto the ice. They were elated as they excitedly examined their prey. 'An elderly female,' Ituko announced, pointing to the animal's decayed and broken teeth. After sharpening their knives, they began skinning and butchering the bear while I brewed some tea. They cut the skin in half. 'My son will have his first polar-bear-skin trousers,' Ituko said proudly, as he folded his share of the pelt. The meat too was divided up between them. Only the liver, which because of its high vitamin A content is poisonous to both dogs and humans, was discarded by Ituko, who tossed it into the water.

We were beginning to load the meat onto the sleds when Ituko suddenly crouched and pointed out across the ice. 'Nanuq,' he whispered excitedly. Four hundred yards away there was another polar bear. It was approaching us, slowly following our tracks. Every so often it would stop, raise its head and scent the air before continuing again. Jens was quick to act. Leaving Ituko to finish loading the meat, he ran over to his sled and released several of his dogs. Then he grabbed his whip and drove his dogsled towards the bear. The sea-ice was smooth with little snow, and Jens' dogs quickly caught up with the bear. Within a matter of a few minutes the dogs held the bear at bay and Jens shot it dead.

Ituko and Jens were delighted with their success and the process of skinning and butchering began all over again. It was midnight by the time all the meat from the second bear was loaded onto the sleds, and with everything securely lashed down we began to retrace our tracks. Our sleds, which were so heavily laden with meat, made the going slow and it was 3 am by the time we reached the place where we had discarded the supplies and equipment at the start of the chase. I was very tired and much relieved when Ituko and Jens decided to camp nearby. The dogs were tethered to the ice and fed an enormous meal of bear meat, a rare treat. It was a bitterly cold night and inside the tent the three of us gradually thawed out around a primus stove. We drank hot tea and ate several chunks of freshly boiled bear meat before turning in for the night.

We slept in late the next morning. I was relieved that Ituko and Jens didn't want to make an early start. As we drank our morning tea, they seemed happy basking in the success of the previous day. Throughout the morning we all had to make hurried dashes from the tent as we paid the price for having eaten too much polar-bear fat. Apart from tasting good, I discovered that polar-bear fat is a remarkably efficient laxative. The dogs lay sprawled out in the sunshine, still bloated from the previous night's meal. In the afternoon they seemed unenthusiastic at the prospect of being on the move again as we packed the sleds and set off once more.

Ituko prepares to skin a bear out on the ice of Melville Bay.

For the next three days, we travelled the ice of Melville Bay searching for more polar bears. Wherever possible, we kept to smooth ice because our heavily laden sleds now weighed around 1,100 pounds, a heavy load for the dogs to pull. Though we came across numerous sets of tracks, we saw no bears. On one occasion when we were retracing our tracks we discovered that a polar bear had been following us – the hunted following the hunters.

We also came across the site of a polar bear's kill. Ituko showed me round the area like a detective at the scene of a crime. 'The bear killed the seal here,' he said, standing by a seal's breathing-hole that was iced over and tinged with blood. 'He dragged it over here and ate it,' he said, moving on to a heavily bloodstained area of ice. 'Then the bear had a sleep over there,' he continued, pointing to a hollowed area of snow by a pressure ridge. 'And here,' he said finally, pointing to a pile of black excrement, 'the bear had a shit. You see,' he said respectfully, 'polar bears are hunters just like us!'

We awoke early on 30 March to a dramatic change in the weather. It was overcast and much warmer, with a strong wind blowing from the southeast. Ituko announced that we would not hunt today because it was Easter Sunday, so we spent the morning relaxing around the camp. We ate biscuits and drank some hot chocolate that I had been saving for special occasions. Ituko asked me what I thought about ending the hunt and heading back home to Moriussaq. 'You are the boss,' I replied. 'No,' Ituko said, shaking his head, 'my son Igaja is the boss, I want to see him again.' By now our supplies were dwindling and the weather was deteriorating, so it seemed as good a time as any to begin heading back.

By the early afternoon it was obvious that Ituko wanted to be on the move, and so we abandoned our day of Easter rest. We broke camp, packed the sleds, hitched up the dogs and began the journey back to land. Two hours later Ituko spotted a polar bear and suddenly 'home' was the last thing on our minds. We quickly unpacked the sleds again to lighten them and the chase began. Luck was on our side. Within an hour Jens had caught up with it and we had our third bear of the hunt, a large male. Ituko and Jens were ecstatic. They chatted and laughed like a couple of schoolboys as they skinned and butchered the bear. With that diversion over, we continued our journey towards the coast, which was still about a day's travel away. We pressed on until dusk and then made camp.

I awoke the following morning to the sound of the tent flapping in the wind. We had bad weather again. It was stormy and snowing quite hard with the visibility down to about 50 yards. Despite the bad weather, we broke camp and continued our journey, heading northeast. Soon a large lead barred our way, forcing us to turn east. The pressure-ice gradually became worse and worse, with high ridges often only a few yards apart. Manoeuvring the heavy sleds over the very rough ice proved tiring and slow for both us and the dogs. It seemed to take ages just to go a few yards. On one occasion when Jens' sled overturned we had to unload it in order to get it the right way up. To make matters worse, one of Ituko's dogs, called Skidoo, was on heat, and her main suitor, Alligator, was constantly picking fights with any other male that showed any interest in her. The last thing we needed while trying to cross rough pressure-ice was a dogfight.

The husky's wolf ancestry shows at feeding time.

Travelling along the frozen coast near Cape York at sunset.

'Sometimes I wish I had a real skidoo,' Ituko said to me, as once again his dog-team dissolved into one large ball of snarling fur. I asked him whether he thought a skidoo would be able to pull a 1,100-pound sled over these high pressure ridges, but my question was academic as the Inughuit have always banned the use of skidoos for hunting in Avanersuaq. This measure, which was implemented by the local hunters council, was designed both to preserve the culture of the Inughuit and to conserve the region's game.

In the afternoon the low cloud occasionally lifted, giving us a brief misty glimpse of a cape or headland before it was obscured once again by cloud and falling snow. It was good to see land again, and Ituko and Jens tried to work out our position. Neither recognized any landmarks and figured that we were somewhere south of Savissivik.

We pressed on slowly eastward over the rough ice. Just before dusk the weather began to clear, and we discovered that we were not as far south as we had thought, but halfway between Savissivik and Ivnaanganeq (Cape York). A short while later, we reached smooth landfast ice, much to everyone's relief. After a tea-break, and having untangled the dogs' traces, we headed towards Ivnaanganeq.

It was 1 am when we finally reached the cape. Ituko and Jens tethered their dogs on the sea-ice. To our disappointment, we discovered that the hut there was empty and cold. It was still Easter and the hunters were probably all at home in Savissivik. Ituko and Jens were quick to lay claim to the only two mattresses in the hut. I made it clear that I was happy to sleep on my caribou skin. I jokingly told them that Kullorsuaq hunters would have been using the mattresses, so they were probably infested with fleas. We all ended up sleeping on our own caribou skins again that night.

It was stormy again the next morning and every muscle in my body ached after the tiring sledging of the previous day. While we waited for the wind to drop, Ituko and Jens fed their teams. By mid-afternoon the weather had improved and we began the long journey back to Moriussaq. The conditions were good and there was not too much snow on the ice to slow down our heavy sleds.

After another two days' travelling, we stopped at Umivik, the most easterly tip of Saunders Island, to make tea. We were all in high spirits, as we were only about three hours from Moriussaq. I reminded Ituko of the day I had visited him in Moriussaq and how he had jokingly predicted that we would catch three polar bears. 'Maybe I am an *angakkuq* [shaman],' he replied jokingly with a happy grin on his face. Over tea, Ituko told me that as we arrived at Moriussaq I should shout out the traditional Inughuit cry of '*Nanoqihuguut*' ('We've got a bear'). He made me repeat it numerous times until I had got the pronunciation correct. In the event it was hardly necessary, as we were spotted while we were still far out on the ice, and the Inughuit could tell from our laden sleds that we had had a successful hunt. As we approached the village, figures emerged from its small cluster of houses and gathered down on the shoreline to greet us.

That evening the whole village was invited to a celebratory meal of boiled polar-bear meat. They crammed into Jens' small hut, until it was bursting at the seams, to hear Ituko and Jens recount the events of the past few weeks. Later, as Ituko relaxed

A polar-bear skin stretched out on a drying-frame outside a house in Savissivik.

at his home cradling his baby son in his arms, he told me, 'I was so happy today as we left Umivik that I was frightened I would die before I reached Moriussaq.'

By now, I too was thinking of home. I called Thule airbase the next morning and managed to get a seat on a military flight to Sondre Stromfjord in South Greenland for the following day. From there I could connect with flights to Copenhagen and London. When I told Ituko he immediately offered to take me to the base by dogsled and we left later that day. After our long hunt, it was a relaxing and easy journey.

It was almost dark by the time we passed Uummannaq Mountain and the lights of the airbase shone ahead of us at the bottom of North Star Bay. After two months in the quiet and beauty of a North Greenland winter, the airbase, with its trucks, buses and ugly barrack buildings, seemed like a very different world. There I telephoned for a car to take me to the North Star Inn. I said goodbye to Ituko and watched as he and his dogs disappeared into the darkness of North Star Bay.

I turned around to see headlights approaching and a pickup truck pulled up alongside me. I threw my baggage in the back and climbed in beside the driver, a large bearded Dane. 'Where have you come from?' he asked, looking at me as though I had just arrived from another planet. When I told him Moriussaq, he just shrugged and said, 'Never heard of it.' I explained that it was a village about 20 miles north of the base. He said that he had been working on the base for three years and had never visited any of the local communities. 'Everything I need is here,' he explained, 'restaurant, bar, clubs, bowling. Besides, what is there to see out there? Just a few villages full of drunken Eskimos.'

The Cree of the Canadian Sub-Arctic

Gifts from the North Wind

The Cree Indians of northern Quebec belong to the Algonquian linguistic group. Their ancestors are thought to have first settled on the east side of James Bay some 4,000 years ago. These early settlers lived as nomads, eking out an existence from the sparse resources that the *taiga* had to offer, by hunting, trapping and fishing.

The seventeenth century brought to this area the first European explorers, such as Henry Hudson, who arrived in 1610. These were followed by traders who were keen to exploit the furs that the region had to offer. These traders relied on close collaboration with the Cree. The traders would have found it very difficult to survive without assistance from the Cree who knew the land and were excellent trappers. Both sides benefitted from the relationship. The fur-traders introduced guns, metal objects and string which were useful to the Cree, while they themselves were quick to adopt certain aspects of Cree technology, such as snowshoes and canoes.

Small settlements were established, mainly along the coast of James Bay, and gradually these became the permanent homes for the Cree. Their livelihood, however, remained in the 'bush', where they hunted, trapped and fished far into the interior. The animals most highly valued by Cree hunters were moose, caribou and wild geese.

ABOVE *Johnny, grandson of Abel and Elizabeth Brien, peers out of the family's tent.*

LEFT *In autumn sunshine, Elizabeth Brien holds a beaver skin stretched onto a drying-frame.*

Today, there are around 10,000 Cree in the James Bay area, living in nine main communities. Their territory is vast, ranging from Whapmagoostui (formerly 'Great Whale') in the north to Waswanipi in the south. Most Cree live close to the coast of James Bay, but there are also several inland communities.

The land that the Cree live on was part of the unilateral grant by Charles II of England to the Hudson Bay Company in 1670. It was later transferred to the Dominion of Canada after confederation, before being claimed by the government of the Province of Quebec. The Cree see history differently. As far as they were concerned, they had never relinquished the aboriginal rights to their ancestral lands. For years they witnessed increasing misuse of their homeland by white men, as mining, forestry and hydro-electric schemes encroached onto their land.

So when, in 1971, Quebec's prime minister Bourassa announced a vast hydro-electric project that entailed flooding 68,000 square miles of northern Quebec's boreal forest and tundra the Cree successfully defended their traditional lands by opposing the scheme in the courts. The affair was settled by negotiation which culminated in the signing of the James Bay and Northern Quebec Agreement in 1975. Under this agreement, the Cree and most of Quebec's Inuit relinquished their claims to the province's northern lands in return for 225 million Canadian dollars and 5,400 square miles of native land reserves, as well as exclusive hunting, fishing and trapping rights to a further 60,000 square miles.

This was not the end of the matter, however, as in 1989 the Cree went to the courts again to try to stop a second phase of hydro-electric development in their territory, on the grounds that it breached the former James Bay Agreement and that it would result in an environmental catastrophe. Their campaign was successful and resulted in Quebec's nationalist premier, Jacques Parizeau, shelving the $13 billion project, 'for the foreseeable future', in November 1994.

Today, the Cree continue to hunt and trap on their lands, but despite their success in the courts the threat of further hydro-electric development in the future still hangs over them.

. . . .

A stiff northerly breeze put a bite in the air, heralding the approach of winter. It was early October in the Cree community of Mistassini, and, from a jetty at the lakeside, I climbed into the front of an old De Havilland Otter and strapped myself in beside the Cree pilot, Paul Petawabano. I glanced behind me; the fuselage was stacked from the floor to the roof with boxes of provisions and equipment. Crammed in among all this cargo sat Abel Brien, his wife Elizabeth and their grandson Johnny. Abel and his family were leaving to spend the winter at their camp by Lake Bourinot, some 200 miles north of Mistassini.

Abel holds the pelts of his autumn catch of pine martens.

Paul started the engine and went through his pre-flight checks. 'This plane is 40 years old,' he told me as he taxied the plane away from the jetty and out into Lake Mistassini. The age of the plane didn't worry me in the least. The De Havilland Otter, and its smaller contemporary the Beaver, were classic workhorses of the North. Nowadays, they may be, as a pilot friend of mine described them, 'spare parts flying in formation', but somehow these planes just seem to keep on flying. Anyway, I felt in good hands. Paul had been a bush pilot for 25 years and in 1982 formed his own airline, Waasheshkun ('clear skies') Airways, at Mistassini.

Paul opened up the throttle and we began to gather speed across the surface of the lake. A minute later we were airborne and began to head north towards Abel's camp. Mistassini looked larger than I expected from the air. Up until the early 1960s it had consisted of only two houses, a Hudson's Bay Company store and a church. Then the Cree only lived there during the summer months, when they put up their tents along the lake shore. Each autumn they left, and headed for their winter hunting-grounds. Today, Mistassini has a growing population of around 3,000, and is the largest of the James Bay Cree communities.

Elizabeth lays a carpet of spruce twigs on a tent floor.

Mistassini was the last sign of human habitation we were to see from the air. As we flew north there were no more villages, no roads; only the wilderness of the Canadian Shield with its seemingly endless spruce forests, rivers, and myriad small lakes. After two hours of flying, Paul pointed out Lake Bourinot ahead of us and we began to make our descent. A few minutes later we landed on the lake close to Abel's camp. As we got into shallow water close to the shore, Paul and Abel each grabbed a paddle, climbed out onto the floats and paddled the plane to the shore. Abel's son Alex and his daughter-in-law Harriet had arrived in another plane from Mistassini shortly beforehand, and they helped us unload the supplies and equipment from the aircraft.

This was a remote spot, even by Canadian wilderness standards. It was also very beautiful. The lake was fringed by spruce forest and the clusters of willow near the water's edge had been turned golden brown by the autumn frosts.

The camp was situated near a small promontory on the lakeside. There were a couple of canoes, some oildrums and a fish-smoking rack. In a small clearing, set back from the water's edge, there was also a partially built log cabin that Abel had begun the previous summer. This coming winter would probably be the last in which Abel and his family would live in tents.

We carried the supplies and equipment from the shore, and erected two canvas-walled tents: one for Alex and Harriet, and the other for Abel, Elizabeth, Johnny and myself. While Abel and Alex cut some suitable poles for the tent, Elizabeth and Harriet walked off into the forest behind the camp; they appeared later carrying huge bundles of spruce twigs, which they painstakingly laid as a thick carpet on the tent floor. These spruce twigs, I discovered, were not only soft and warm to lie on but were also very fragrant, and my sleeping bag smelt of pine for months afterwards.

By mid-afternoon we had just about finished making camp. We collected some firewood and Abel set up the transceiver which enabled him to keep contact with Mistassini and other winter camps. The weather was wonderful and there were none of the mosquitoes and black flies that plague the Sub-Arctic during the summer months. We sat outside in the warm afternoon sunshine, drinking coffee and eating bannock.

We had brought little fresh meat with us, so Alex and Harriet made the most of the fine weather and went off hunting in one of the canoes. Abel and Elizabeth took the other canoe and went to set a fish net out on the lake. Later, as the sun set, the colour of the sky reflected pink on the still surface of the lake. The temperature fell sharply once the sun had dropped below the horizon, but inside our tent it was cosy with the wood stove burning. Alex and Harriet arrived back just before dark, empty-handed but excited at having seen a black bear in the distance. Alex had tried to follow it, but it had eluded him.

In the evening, Abel spoke on the radio with friends at other bush camps, and Elizabeth prepared a meal of goose for us all. The James Bay Cree hunt migrating geese as they fly through their territory in the spring and autumn. Geese are an important source of meat for the Cree, and it is estimated that these goose-hunts provide the coastal communities with four months' supply of meat each year.

After the meal we relaxed in the tent. Abel told me that he had been coming here with his family to their winter hunting-grounds for 30 years. In the old days they travelled from Mistassini each autumn by canoe, which took about six weeks. Today, the journey had taken us only two hours. Their family's hunting-grounds are a designated area of approximately 1,500 square miles. I was surprised to learn how systematic Abel's hunting and trapping activities were. He divides his land into two separate areas, hunting and trapping in each in alternate years. This allows the game populations to recover.

LEFT A pine marten.

OPPOSITE Portrait of Abel, taken during an autumn hunting-trip.

Abel was relaxed and obviously pleased to be back. 'I feel like a prisoner who has just been released from jail,' he told me. When he is away from his hunting-grounds in the late spring and summer months, Abel guides sport fishermen and takes other work, such as tree-felling, whenever he can get it. Now he was back in his element and looking forward to the winter trapping season that lay ahead.

Alex told me that he and Harriet were going to be here for about ten days. This last-minute decision of Alex and Harriet to stay and help his father was a great help to me, as they both spoke good English whereas Elizabeth and Abel spoke very little.

Abel, I soon discovered, was an early riser. The next morning he was up before daybreak and had lit the stove and made coffee before anyone else had stirred. The weather had changed; it was heavily overcast with snow flurries.

During the morning Abel and Elizabeth went to check the fish net that they had set the previous day. Several of the net's floats had been dragged under the surface of the water, indicating a good catch. Elizabeth kept the canoe in position while Abel worked his way along the net removing the fish. In the end, they had caught an assortment of about 20 fish. There were a few lake trout, wall eye, northern pike and white fish, but the majority were suckers. Elizabeth told me that the Cree name for Lake Bourinot translates as 'Sucker Lake'.

The next day, the weather was still heavily overcast and a light breeze brought more flurries of fine snow. The view from our camp was monochromatic. The lake, the trees and the sky all appeared in varying shades of grey. Abel was going hunting again and he invited me to join him. He travelled remarkably light, carrying only a rifle, a hatchet, and a canvas shoulder-bag, containing traps and other hunting accessories. We crossed to the east side of Lake Bourinot and then made a short portage to another lake. Heading along the south side of the lake, Abel suddenly changed direction, steering the canoe towards the shore. 'Kaakuush [bear],' said Abel, pointing towards a trail leading from the lake. We hauled the canoe up onto dry land, and then Abel began to follow the tracks into the forest. Every so often he stopped and crouched to examine

Abel and Elizabeth check their fish net on Lake Bourinot.

Elizabeth lays some white fish out on racks for smoking at the camp.

them. They were black bear tracks, a few days old. He returned to the canoe for a large steel trap, which he set just off the trail close to a fallen tree. This he baited with peanut butter and chainsaw oil, a combination that bears apparently find irresistible. Abel carefully covered the trap with small spruce branches and then we continued our journey paddling close to shore. A solitary muskrat swimming in the distance was one of the few signs of life.

In the middle of the day we went ashore again, and, after some hot tea and bannock, Abel led the way up a hill that rose behind the lake. He was tall and powerfully built, and for a man in his 50s he could sustain an astonishing pace. Even through thick bush I had a job keeping up with him. From the top of the hill Abel scanned the surrounding area through his binoculars, but there was no sign of any caribou or moose. We returned to the canoe and continued paddling for what seemed miles and miles. Abel paddled a canoe in the same way as he walked, with seemingly endless energy. After another two portages, I was relieved when I spotted our camp at Lake Bourinot.

Elizabeth had hot coffee on the stove waiting for us. Soon after our return, Alex and Harriet arrived back, also empty-handed. I was surprised that we had seen so little wildlife. Alex assured me that, once the first snow settled and we could see the animal tracks, things would improve. In the late afternoon, Abel took one of the canoes to a camp on the other side of the lake to look for an axe he had dropped the previous winter. He arrived back just before dark without the axe, but carrying a beaver he had shot.

Abel decided to celebrate the first catch of the winter trapping season with a 'feast'. I had expected him to skin the beaver, but as this was a special occasion he built a fire and singed off all the fur, effectively sending 45 Canadian dollars up in smoke. 'The skin tastes very good', he told me. The beaver was cut up, boiled and laid out on a makeshift table in the uncompleted cabin, together with some cakes, steam pudding and doughnuts. Feast did seem an apt description of the occasion as there seemed to be a massive amount of food. Like everyone else, I took a chunk of the steaming-hot beaver meat. I was waiting for it to cool when Elizabeth suddenly grabbed it from my plate and

LEFT Abel paddles his canoe while out hunting in the autumn.

OPPOSITE Elizabeth prepares a beaver for cooking at her camp on Lake Bourinot.

substituted it for another piece of meat. Alex must have seen the expression of surprise on my face, and quickly offered an explanation. I had taken a leg, a part of the beaver that according to Cree tradition must only be eaten by women. The Cree believe that if a man eats meat from a beaver's leg Chuetenshu, the north wind and lord of all the animals will freeze his feet. Some other animals that the Cree hunt, such as bear, otter and porcupine, also have parts that can only be eaten by one gender or the other.

Traditionally, the Cree believe that animals have intelligence and character, as well as souls and spirits, in the same way that people do. The Cree also believe that the animals they catch are a gift from Chuetenshu and give themselves willingly to the hunter. These 'gifts' place a hunter under an obligation to cause the animal no unnecessary suffering, and to follow certain procedures, which include completely using the flesh and all other useful parts. Failure to observe these procedures results in

the hunter being punished either by Chuetenshu or by the animals, who will no longer allow themselves to be caught. From the Cree viewpoint, the animal's body feeds the hunter and his family, while the animal's spirit returns to be reborn. By sacrificing themselves, animals enable humans to live. In return, careful hunting maintains healthy wildlife populations. The animals are killed but their numbers are not diminished and in this way both the hunter and the hunted can flourish. The Cree see this process as not totally one-sided, because when humans die their bodies too become food for other living things.

The difference in attitude between Cree and white hunters was brought home to me during my first few days in northern Quebec. I had gone to the town of Chibougamau with several Cree from Mistassini to buy provisions. As we made our way along the main street we passed a parked truck; lashed to its roof-rack was the decapitated head of a recently killed moose. Blood had dripped and congealed on the roof and windscreen. 'Why do you white people do that?' one of the Cree said to me, pointing to the grotesque hunting trophy. 'You should respect the animals you hunt.'

Abel and Elizabeth had appeared to have wholeheartedly embraced Christianity, so I was surprised to discover that they still observed some of the traditional Cree spiritual taboos.

Recently we had not been successful at finding any large game near our camp, so Abel decided to look further afield. On 10 October we broke camp early, and loaded camping equipment and supplies into the two canoes. Then we set off, heading south down Lake Bourinot. It was a fine sunny morning with a strong northerly breeze that rippled the surface of the lake. When we reached the southern end of the lake we emptied the canoes and hauled them out of the water for what was to be the first of many portages. It was tiring work. First we dragged the canoes through thick bush that was often waist-high to the next lake. Then we had to carry all the equipment and supplies. These portages varied in length from 100 yards to half a mile. Walking through the thick bush was too much for Abel's young grandson, Johnny. The willow bushes were almost as tall as he was, so Abel carried him on his shoulders.

In the early afternoon, we stopped to rest and have something to eat. We were just about to move on again when Alex spotted a group of caribou grazing near some trees on the far side of the lake. He and Abel discussed tactics, then they grabbed their rifles and quickly got into one of the canoes and paddled slowly and quietly across the lake. At the far side they crawled up the bank on all fours. They were down-wind of the caribou, which was in their favour, and they began slowly to stalk the grazing animals. I watched through binoculars as they moved cautiously towards their prey. After half an hour they seemed so close that I found it hard to believe that the caribou had not seen them. Hunters in the south usually wear well-camouflaged clothing when they hunt deer. In spite of the fact that he was wearing a bright red checked shirt, Alex was able to get within about 50 yards of the caribou without them seeing him. Abel and

During a portage on an autumn hunting-trip, Abel carried Johnny.

Alex both fired at the animals almost simultaneously and two of the caribou staggered and fell. The remaining caribou panicked and ran. Two, however, made the mistake of running right towards Abel and Alex. More shots rang out, and they too fell to the ground.

Everyone was delighted, because we badly needed the meat. Abel and Alex skinned and butchered the caribou. By the time they had finished it was late in the afternoon, so Abel decided that we should make camp nearby. Later we roasted chunks of caribou meat on sticks over an open fire and cooked bannock the same way. Abel boiled up the leg bones, which he then split with a hatchet, and we ate the marrow. The night was bitterly cold, so we took refuge inside the tent, where as always it was snug from the heat of the wood-burning stove.

Peering out of the tent the next morning, we were greeted by the all-too-familiar leaden skies and falling snow which swirled in the blustery wind. Abel and Alex cached most of the caribou meat, as having to carry it on portages would slow us down. Later, we loaded up the canoes and set off, but the driving rain made it miserable as we headed towards the Eastmain river. After two long and tiring portages, Abel decided to abandon travelling in these conditions and once again we made camp.

A couple of hours later we were relaxing in the tent, eating bannock and drinking hot coffee with our wet clothes hanging up to dry near the stove. At dusk the walls of the tent began to flap as the wind strengthened. Abel went outside for more firewood and came back covered in snow. I had already seen how fast the weather can change in this part of the world, so if it was bad now, I reasoned, there was every chance we would wake to fine weather again tomorrow.

I was wrong. The next morning the weather was even worse. Wet blowing snow reduced the visibility to just a few yards. We spent the entire day in the tent with the radio on, listening as people at different camps called each other to exchange news. There are about 53 bush camps in the Mistassini region with two to three families at each camp. The radio is the only way that they have to keep in touch with each other. It seemed that the bad weather was widespread, and at most camps people were just sitting it out. There was a humorous moment when the radio came to life and an excited voice announced, 'Some geese have landed right by my camp. I will let you know how many I get.' The radio went quiet for a while, then the same voice, sounding disappointed and rather subdued, said, 'none.'

The following morning the weather had improved and Abel decided that we should head back to Lake Bourinot. We broke camp and were on the move by 10 am. A blanket of snow had transformed the landscape. This was to be a mixed blessing, as it made it easier for us to drag the canoes overland but harder to trudge through the snow carrying our equipment and supplies. By now, ice had begun to form around the edges of the lakes.

Communication between Abel and myself was difficult because of our limited understanding of each other's languages; misunderstandings were inevitable. On one occasion, Abel was in a canoe at the edge of a lake breaking ice while I steadied it from the bank. He turned to me and said what I thought was 'push', so I gave the canoe a good shove. As it slid away it rocked violently, and Abel fought to keep his balance. For a second I thought he was going to fall in, but he managed to steady himself at the very last moment. Obviously disgruntled, he muttered something at me in Cree. A few moments later, Alex arrived on the scene. There was an exchange of words and it was obvious Abel was not happy. Alex turned to me and asked, 'What did my father say to you?' I explained that he had told me to push and that I had given the canoe a strong shove. Alex began to laugh, explaining, 'My father didn't say "push", he said "boos", which means "get in".'

We reached our camp shortly before dark. By then I was tired and relieved to be back. I was also pleased to have the opportunity of using the 'camp bath'. It consisted of half of a 40-gallon fuel drum which we partially filled with buckets of water heated on the stove.

OVERLEAF Spruce trees covered by the first snow of winter at the edge of Lake Bourinot.

BELOW Once the lakes begin to freeze in the autumn, canoe travel becomes difficult.

The next morning we awoke to find our camp enshrouded in freezing fog, but as the sun burnt through it turned into a magical morning. The trees around the lake were covered by hoar-frost, and the snow sparkled in the sunshine. In the afternoon I went with Abel to check the bear trap we had set a few days earlier. It was much harder to get there this time; ice around the lake had thickened to the extent that we couldn't break it with our paddles or canoe. We had to abandon the canoe a long way from the trap and hike in through the bush. To my relief, there was no bear or any tracks nearby.

RIGHT Elizabeth gives Johnny a bath in a tent at their winter camp.

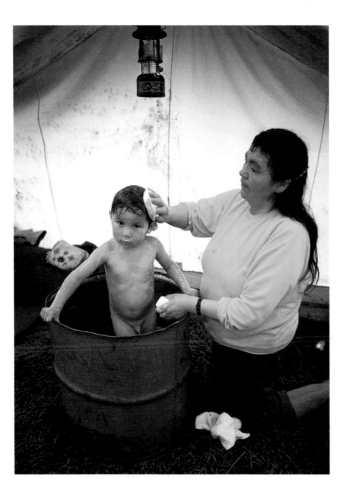

OPPOSITE Elizabeth picking cranberries near her camp in the autumn.

It was late in the season and by now most of the black bears would have begun their hibernation for the winter. Abel sprung the trap with a stick and carried it back to the canoe. As we returned to camp, we spotted a beaver lodge at the mouth of a small stream. We stopped, and Abel set a trap.

Over the next few days, the weather deteriorated once again. We fell into a routine of checking traps and fish nets as well as collecting firewood and working on the new cabin. On one of the few days when the rain and sleet let up for a while, we went down the lakeside by canoe and spent the afternoon picking cranberries. We ended up filling a couple of plastic buckets, and back at the camp we gorged ourselves on the delicious berries which we ate with some of Elizabeth's freshly made hot bannock.

After waiting several days for the weather to improve, we got a call over the radio to tell us that Paul Petawabano was planning to fly to our camp that day. It was time for Alex and Harriet to leave for Mistassini. While they packed, Abel took one of the canoes out onto the lake to break the newly formed ice so that the plane would be able to land.

In the early afternoon, we heard the plane approaching and dashed from the tent in time to see it land on the lake. It brought Abel and Elizabeth's 18-year-old daughter, Doreen, who had come to help her parents, as well as three months' supply of flour (300 pounds) and other supplies. Alex and Harriet took much of the caribou meat with them back to Mistassini to distribute among their family and friends. Sharing is still an intrinsic part of Cree life, and much of the 'bush food' finds its way back into the communities through a complicated food-sharing network.

Once the plane had disappeared from view, Elizabeth told me of her disappointment that neither of her two sons wanted to overwinter with them. 'They say it's too expensive to come here, but they both have new cars,' she told me. Like many young Cree, Alex seemed to prefer the bright lights of Mistassini to life at a bush camp.

Later that day, we prepared to move to another campsite on the other side of the lake. Abel had wintered there since he was a boy and Elizabeth told me it would be warmer and more comfortable. She was right. Abel had constructed a spacious canvas winter tent with wooden sides to protect it from the wind. Close by was a smaller tent that the family used for smoking meat.

The clutter of hunting equipment around the camp suggested many years of use. Abel had made a large wood-burning stove from a fuel drum, which proved very efficient. Elizabeth fried up some caribou meat for our evening meal, but Johnny was more interested in the cookies and candy that Doreen had brought from Mistassini.

The following days were characterized by bad weather. With the new snow on the ground, animal tracks became visible by the lakeside. Whenever we came across new tracks, Abel studied them carefully and would sometimes set a trap close by. It was not long before Abel returned to camp with another beaver. Elizabeth quickly skinned it and Abel prepared to roast the meat, stretching the carcass by using several small pieces of wood. He then suspended it from the roof so that it hung close to the stove, and slowly roasted in the heat. I found beaver meat much more enjoyable roasted rather than boiled.

Towards the end of October, the ice on the lakes was too thick to travel by canoe, but still too thin to drive a snowmobile on. Abel hunted and trapped on foot. He would often be up and gone before daybreak, covering considerable distances in a day, and he rarely came back much before dusk. Elizabeth trapped too, setting a series of traps for marten around our camp, which she checked every day. They were baited with caribou meat or fish, and then she would spread 'Right Guard' deodorant onto nearby branches to act as a lure. I wondered how they had discovered that this was effective.

Abel removes a beaver he has caught from one of his traps.

It snowed most days and it began to look as though the bad weather was endless. When we were not hunting and trapping, there was always plenty of work to do around camp; collecting water and cutting and hauling firewood were never-ending chores. Some days Abel would fell spruce trees with his chainsaw, and the rest of us would use axes to cut off the branches before he cut the trunk into suitably sized logs for the stove. Abel and Elizabeth were both masterful at wielding an axe; by comparison I was totally inept. They were able to split logs with little more than a leisurely tap. I would inevitably end up with the head of the axe firmly embedded in the log and would then spend the next five minutes trying to remove it. If nothing else, I provided some amusement for Abel and his family.

RIGHT **The light from a kerosene lamp illuminates a Cree winter tent at dusk.**

OPPOSITE **Elizabeth chops firewood at the family's winter camp.**

Once the weather began to get too cold to work in the porch of the main tent, Abel and Elizabeth built a smaller tent as a workshop where they cleaned skins and repaired hunting equipment. Abel was a skilled craftsman, and, with a couple of lengths of larch wood and some basic tools, he began to make a pair of new snowshoes. He immersed the wood for the frames in boiling water, so he could bend them to the correct shape. Meanwhile, Elizabeth and Doreen began the long slow job of preparing the caribou hide that would be used for the webbing. They scraped off the excess fat, cut off the hair and washed the hide. They cut it into long thin lengths, before lashing it, while still wet, onto the frames. Then they left it to dry. After a few days, the

webbing was as taut as the strings on a tennis racket. The finished snowshoes were beautiful, and looked as though they had been precision-made by machine, not handcrafted in a tent.

At the end of October, Abel took in the fish net. He would set it again once the lake ice was thick enough to walk on, but in the mean time we would have to rely on meat. We still had a little smoked caribou left, but we needed more fresh meat. Day after day Abel hunted for caribou without success. Fortunately, he managed to catch enough beaver and otter for us to get by on. I was to have another interesting insight into Cree taboos when, one evening, Elizabeth apologized to me for serving a meal of otter for the third day running. 'We can't waste the meat or we won't be able to catch another one,' she explained, 'If we threw it away the otters would know, they are clever.' I didn't find otter an unpleasant meat, so it didn't bother me in the least having to eat it three days running.

One day Abel returned with a porcupine. Elizabeth was delighted as he didn't catch them often and the fatty meat

was something of a delicacy. She ate the head, because one of the Cree traditions stipulates that a porcupine's head must be eaten by a woman. 'In the old days,' Abel told me as he scraped the last bit of meat off one of the porcupine's shoulder blades. 'we would hang this bone up close to the stove and then someone in the tent would receive knowledge of where the caribou were.' I suggested that we try it, but Elizabeth refused. It was incompatible with her Christian beliefs.

The 11th of November is a holiday in the region. It marks the signing of the James Bay Agreement. One of the benefits for the Crees that came out of this agreement was an income-support programme which enabled hunters like Abel to

ABOVE Elizabeth threads caribou-hide lacing onto a new pair of snowshoes.

LEFT Sam Edwards scraping a caribou hide that has been pegged out to dry.

claim subsidies to help finance their hunting activities. It was not holiday weather. We watched as storm-force winds blew clouds of snow across the frozen surface of the lake. It may have been a public holiday in Mistassini, but Abel had us all working in the forest, cutting and stacking firewood which he later hauled back to our camp by snowmobile.

By the second week in November, there was deep snow on the land and the ice on the lakes was thick enough to drive a snowmobile on. This increased Abel's hunting range dramatically. Elizabeth told me that, in the old days before snowmobiles, Abel would sometimes be gone for nine days at a time, leaving her alone at the camp with their three children. When she had to go to the forest to collect wood, she used to tie up the young children to one of the tent-poles so they would not come to any harm while she was away.

Abel hunted almost every day except Sundays, usually on day trips, leaving at dawn and returning at dusk. Sometimes, when he hunted further away from the camp, he would be gone for two or three days at a time. I often went with him, riding on the narrow birchwood sled he pulled behind his snowmobile, or sometimes driving his

Abel travelling by skidoo to check his trapline in November.

Watched by her grandson, Elizabeth spends an evening sewing at the camp.

second snowmobile. It was getting much colder now, and Elizabeth kitted me out with
a pair of moccasins lined with duffel socks. These were very comfortable to walk in,
and my feet seldom got cold. Hunting-trips with Abel were usually long and tiring. We
normally travelled from one watercourse to another, checking his traps along the way,
and setting more whenever we encountered a new beaver lodge or fresh marten tracks.
I soon discovered that driving a snowmobile through spruce forests, where the trees
were close together and the snow was soft and deep, was tiring and required much
more skill than driving across the hard-packed snow of open tundra which I had done
in other areas of the North. The answer, it seemed, was to keep the 'revs up' and
always keep moving; the moment I stopped, the machine would sink deeper and
deeper into the snow and get stuck. Then I would be faced with the task of standing
waist-deep in snow trying to lift the machine out of the pit it had dug for itself.

    After a few days in the bush, it was good to get back to the relative comfort of our
main camp. The tent was warm and Elizabeth or Doreen would always prepare a hot
meal for us in the evenings. Elizabeth worked very hard, and, even as we relaxed, she
would be sewing or cleaning skins by the light of a kerosene lamp as she listened to
gospel music. Until we went to sleep the transceiver was always kept on standby. Most
evenings there would be a lot of chatting between people at the different bush camps.
Everyone wanted to know the latest news and how the hunting and trapping was going
elsewhere. Sometimes, when the radio reception was bad, messages had to be relayed
from camp to camp.

Occasionally, I too would get called on the radio for a chat. Some of the Cree were obviously intrigued by my presence at a winter camp and wondered what I thought of life in the bush. In the end I was on friendly terms with several trappers, whom, regrettably, I never got the chance to meet. One of the regulars I talked with was Charlie, who was camped at Indicator Lake. He had a sense of humour and I knew that whenever I spoke to him there would be some smart comment at my expense. 'I hear you were out on snowshoes today,' he began on one occasion, before adding, 'they tell me you leave tracks like two people walking side by side.' After the wisecrack, he went on to give me some sound advice on using snowshoes. The pair that Abel lent me were about 5 feet long by 14 inches wide, and were upturned at the front. I was always afraid that when I kicked forward with one snowshoe it would catch and break the front of the other one.

On a number of evenings, as I lay in my sleeping-bag, I heard wolves. Sometimes they sounded distant and only just audible; on other occasions they seemed close by. Doreen was afraid of wolves and they made her anxious. I found it a delightful sound and it somehow reinforced the fact, as if it was needed, that I was in the wilderness. One morning we awoke to discover wolf tracks leading right into the porch of the tent. Abel told me that wolves were increasing in the area. Before, they used to follow the caribou south in the winter and then go back with them when they migrated north in the spring. Now, they were spending the whole year in the area and eating beavers when there were no caribou. That was something Abel was not too pleased about.

Most days Abel returned to our camp with an assortment of animals he had caught in his traps. They were usually beaver, marten, mink, muskrat and the occasional porcupine. His trapping success generated a lot more work for Elizabeth and Doreen. They seemed to be forever working – cleaning skins and tying them on frames to dry, often late in the evening.

Despite Abel's trapping success, there was still no sign of any more caribou, and we were getting short of meat again. We broke into our supplies of white-man's food and for several days we seemed to eat nothing but bannock and 'Kraft Dinner' (this packet macaroni with a cheese sauce has become a popular food among native people of the Canadian North).

By the middle of November, the ice on Lake Bourinot was almost 3 inches thick. Abel and Elizabeth set a net under the ice by making a series of holes in a straight line and then passing a nylon line between them under the ice. The net yielded enough fish on a daily basis to keep us well fed. One day, when we hauled up the fish net, there was a small stone in it from the bottom of the lake that had got caught up in the mesh. Elizabeth took the stone back to the tent and hung it up close to the stove by a piece of string as a talisman. 'It will help us make a kill,' she told me. I thought she must have felt the need for more assistance from the spirit world than when she refused to use the porcupine's shoulder blade as a talisman a week or so earlier.

I don't know whether Elizabeth's talisman worked, or whether it was just a coincidence, but two days later Abel came back from hunting with two caribou, three beaver, three marten, five mink and a broad contented smile.

Among the people that Elizabeth and Abel regularly contacted were Sam Edwards and his wife Jean, whose hunting-land bordered theirs. During one of their radio chats they arranged for the two families to meet at a lake not far from the Edwards' cabin.

We set off on a rare sunny morning. The ice conditions were not good, which made the journey longer than normal; nevertheless we arrived at the lake before the others. Abel quickly began to set his nets, keen to make the most of the opportunity of catching the delicious trout that abounded in the lake. These would make a pleasant change from the suckers that proliferate in Lake Bourinot.

Sam and Jean arrived not long afterwards, together with their granddaughter, Louisa, who was overwintering with them. This meant that Johnny would have company of his own age for a while. The families enjoyed the chance to socialize, and soon everyone was gathered around the fire on the lakeside, roasting chunks of caribou meat on sticks while they chatted.

There was a party atmosphere and news and gossip was exchanged over the crackling of the fire. Despite the sunshine, it was cold, and, after eating, we retired to the Edwards' cabin nearby. It had one main room and a small kitchen area. A large wall-hanging of Christ over their bed left me in little doubt about their religious beliefs.

Also living with them was Sam's brother, Billy. He was a quiet man who could seem gruff and moody at times. Billy hunted and trapped in the traditional way. He didn't have a snowmobile and travelled everywhere on foot, using snowshoes, and hauling a small birchwood sled on which he carried his hunting and trapping gear.

In the evening, Jean prepared a meal of lake trout and bannock, which was followed by a prayer meeting in the cabin. Later, Jean sat on the bed working on a pair of moosehide gauntlets, while she chatted to Elizabeth. Abel, Sam and Billy sat

Elizabeth sets a pan of water to heat above a camp fire.

Sam Edwards checks his fish net, set under the ice of a frozen lake near his camp.

talking in the kitchen area. They seemed to get on well together and enjoy each other's company. There was a lot of news to catch up on. Sam and Abel were still talking when I turned in at 11.30 pm and they were up again talking over coffee at 4.30 am.

We spent one more enjoyable day at Sam and Jean's cabin. The following morning we set off, via the fish nets, back to our camp, having arranged to meet them again in a few days' time at Lake Wehman. The weather was grey and dismal once more, and I was glad when we reached our camp soon after midday.

Later that afternoon, the local representative of the Cree Hunters and Trappers Association at Mistassini broadcast the latest prices over the radio. For the hunters it was not good news. Lynx, mink and beaver pelts were all down considerably. Only marten had stayed the same. The reaction of the Cree hunters over the radio was mixed. There was anger, dismay and bewilderment, but above all they were asking 'Why?'. Some offered possible explanations – 'It must be the animal rights groups . . .' or 'The white men's fur farms that are causing it . . .'

Afterwards, Abel gave a shrug of resignation. 'Even if fur prices continue to fall, I will still spend the winters in the bush,' he told me. Most Cree that I spoke to felt like that. The income they received from selling fur was useful to help finance their life in the bush, but primarily they hunted for food. Abel has been keeping records of his catches on his winter hunting-grounds for the past 30 years. In a typical winter season he would catch around 32 martens, 42 beavers, 10 otters, 12 minks, four muskrats, two wolves and a fox. What I found quite remarkable was just how consistent Abel's catches had been over the years. To maintain such steady figures, he was obviously hunting well within the productivity of these species. It was an indication of good land-management. Abel, like most Cree, markets his furs through the Cree Trappers Association. This organization was set up in 1978 to offer the Cree an alternative to marketing their furs through the Hudson's Bay Company and also to develop trapping-grounds and improve services for trappers. With an office in each of the communities the CTA maintains contact with all of their communities' bush camps. The association is also responsible for monitoring the hunters' catches, so if there is a decline in the population of a particular species they can take whatever action is necessary.

On the morning of 26 November, we prepared to go to Lake Wehman to join Sam, Billy and Jean. We loaded up the sleds with just about everything from our camp that we could move, including the ghetto-blaster, which guaranteed we would be listening to gospel music in the evenings. We left soon after 9 am with both snowmobiles and three sleds. Abel led the way and I followed behind on the second machine.

At Lake Wehman we were met by Billy, who had travelled as usual on snowshoes, hauling his loaded sled behind him. Not long afterwards, Sam and Jean arrived. Abel then set about cutting down some young spruce trees to use as a frame for the two canvas tents, and the camp was constructed with the usual painstaking thoroughness.

Billy Edwards sets out for a day's trapping on snowshoes, hauling a birchwood sled.

By the time we had finished and Elizabeth had laid a floor of spruce branches, the whole process had taken nearly four hours. At dusk we settled down to a meal of caribou, ptarmigan and bannock.

Late in the evening I went outside. It was a cold, clear, moonless night and there was a bright display of Northern Lights which moved across the sky, rippling like a curtain in a gentle breeze. I was standing watching this spectacular array of red and white light when Doreen came up to me. 'We say they are the spirits of our ancestors,' she told me, as we both stood gazing up into the night, 'and if you rub your hands together they will dance in the sky.'

We were to spend the next ten days hunting from the camp. Abel, Sam and Billy all hunted separately. Most days we would be gone soon after dawn and would not return until after dark. Abel hunted hard, and they were long, tiring days. Sometimes when we had travelled far from the camp we would spend the night in a small tent out

A Cessna ski-plane brings supplies to the winter camp of Abel and Elizabeth.

in the bush. Usually, I travelled on the sled that Abel pulled behind his snowmobile. I had to kneel on it because it was only about 14 inches wide. Spending ten hours a day kneeling on the sled as it was pulled over rough terrain played havoc with my knees. For Abel it was a productive time and ten days' trapping yielded three otters, two minks, eight martens, eight beavers, and two porcupines.

By early December, my thoughts were turning to getting home in time for Christmas. There was a problem however, as some unseasonably warm weather had prevented the ice thickening enough on Lake Bourinot. Paul Petawabano needed at least 9 inches of ice on the lake to land his single engine Otter plane on it. The smaller Beaver could land on 7 inches, but the bad news was that we only had about 5 inches of ice at that time. Abel came up with a solution to the problem. There was a Baptist Missionary in Mistassini, called Larry, who had a small Cessna aircraft. He regularly flew to bush camps, and Abel thought it could land on 5 inches of ice without any problem. Abel wanted a plane to come too, as both of his snowmobiles were playing up and his son Alex had offered to lend him his for the rest of the trapping season. The snowmobile could come up on the plane that would collect me.

Alex had spoken to Larry, who had agreed to fly up to Lake Bourinot just as soon as the weather was good enough. Needless to say, no sooner had the arrangements been made than the weather closed in and it snowed hard for the next three days. The weather finally cleared on 8 December. We were expecting Larry to fly up in the morning, and Abel drove his snowmobile up and down the lake to make a landing strip which we marked with spruce branches. Looking at our camp from the lake, there was no mistaking it for anything other than a trappers' camp. There were skins everywhere, an assortment of otter, marten and mink pelts hung on lines to dry, and nearby there were several beaver pelts stretched onto round wooden drying-frames.

Larry left Mistassini just before noon and the various bush camps that he flew over told us of his progress on the radio. It was early afternoon when we finally heard the plane overhead. A short while later, it landed on the ice near our camp. We unloaded the snowmobile and the supplies that Alex had sent up, and then loaded on my gear and some caribou meat for Abel and Elizabeth's family in Mistassini.

I broadcast a quick 'Goodbye' to the other camps over the radio and thanked Abel and Elizabeth. After shaking hands all round, I climbed aboard the plane. Larry was keen to be off. There were low snowclouds to the south, and it would be dark in a couple of hours. Larry told me that he had planned to be here much earlier, but it had been one of those days. 'First I had trouble getting the skis on and then the radio broke', he explained. 'But you managed to fix it?' I asked hopefully. 'No,' came the reply.

Larry opened the throttle and we bumped across the frozen surface of the lake before ascending into the leaden sky. I gazed out at the landscape below, with its snow-covered forests and frozen lakes. It looked very different from when I had flown over it two months before. Then I had wondered how anyone could survive in this vast wilderness. Abel and Elizabeth had showed me how.

The Saami of the Norwegian Arctic
Under the Stars of the Great Bear

The Saami, or Lapps, as they are perhaps better known, have been living in the extreme north of Europe for at least 2,000 years. The exact origins of their culture remain something of a mystery. The first written historical mention of the Saami was made by the Roman historian Tacitus in AD 98. He called them 'Fenni', and described them as being extremely poor, with no weapons, no horses and no houses. He went on to say that their clothes were made of skins and they slept on the bare ground, and women as well as men joined in the hunt.

The region they live in is popularly known as Lapland. It encompasses northern areas of Norway, Sweden, Finland and Russia, with much of it lying above the Arctic Circle. Of the estimated 35,000 Saami living today, around 20,000 are in Norway, 10,000 in Sweden, 3,000 in Finland and 2,000 in Russia. The Saami language belongs to the Finno-Ugrian family of languages, which includes Finnish, Estonian and Hungarian. Considering the size of Lapland, it is not surprising that there are many different regional dialects of the Saami language.

The association between the Saami and reindeer is ancient. Reindeer were one of the first animals to inhabit northern Scandinavia at the end of the last ice age, some

ABOVE *During a hard day's travelling on the spring migration, Johan Logje rests on his snowmobile.*

LEFT *Nils Peter struggles with a reindeer in a corral at their winter pastures at Badasjokka.*

9,000 to 10,000 years ago. When the Saami arrived, they exploited the reindeer for food and clothing. Initially, they just hunted wild reindeer; later, they kept some tamed animals which they used as decoys and transport animals.

During the Middle Ages, some groups of Saami combined hunting wild reindeer with herding domesticated ones. From the seventeenth century, reindeer-hunting was gradually replaced by herding. Though they were kept primarily for their meat and skins, the Saami also milked their reindeer for a large part of the year. The milk was usually made into cheese, which was greatly valued. There is an old Saami saying that the last cheese of one year should see the first cheese of the next. Once shops were established and new foodstuffs were readily available, milking reindeer died out, and today reindeer are kept primarily for meat-production.

Although the Saami in Sweden, Finland and Russia herd reindeer, it is only the 'Mountain Saami' of North Norway who still lead a semi-nomadic lifestyle. They migrate each spring with their reindeer to Finnmark's coastal peninsulas and islands. It is here that the calves are born and the reindeer feed on the rich grass throughout the summer months.

Nowadays, the herders slaughter most of the animals they want to sell for meat while they are still at the coast. Then in the autumn, after the rut, they head inland again, travelling deep into the tundra to their lichen pastures where they spend the winter.

. . . .

Far to the North under the stars of the Great Bear,
our Lapland silently looms;
purple heights beyond shimmering hills,
lake upon lake with their shores aflood;
glittering peaks and ancient grey ridges lift themselves high to the vault of heaven;
the streams rush and the forests sigh;
steel-grey headlands jut into the foaming surf.

(from *The Song of the Saami People* by Isak Saba)

At noon on a clear January day, the full moon had just risen from behind the church at Kautokeino. Apart from the lights which shone in the windows of the houses, the whole village appeared blue in the winter twilight. The two-month-long dark time was nearing an end, and in another couple of weeks the sun would return once more.

At his home on the outskirts of the village, I joined Johan Henrik as he prepared to go to check his reindeer at their winter pastures. It was a cold day and he was warmly dressed in traditional herder's reindeer-skin clothing, with his lasso worn across his chest like a bandolier. Johan Henrik dragged over a small wooden sled and fastened it to his snowmobile. Then, after putting a couple of reindeer skins and a box of food on it, he pulled the starter-cord of the snowmobile several times. Eventually the engine came to life, giving off a cloud of smoke into the cold air. Johan Henrik's dog, Runne, jumped up behind him on the seat and we set off, heading southeast out of Kautokeino.

We sped along a trail that took us through clusters of birch trees and across frozen streams and lakes. Johan Henrik and the other herders had been using this trail all winter and the snow was hard-packed. I was impressed by Runne's sense of balance. He sat bolt upright on the narrow seat, and, despite all the bumps and bends, didn't fall off. It took us about an hour to cover the 20 miles to the area where the herd were, and, not long afterwards, I saw a group of a few hundred reindeer in the distance. Johan Henrik drove slowly towards them, and when we were close he stopped the snowmobile. Most of the reindeer seemed unperturbed by our presence; they carried on feeding on lichen and mosses, clearing away the snow with their hooves.

Johan Henrik walked among the reindeer, with Runne staying obediently by his side. A well-trained dog is invaluable to a reindeer herder, and the Saami mainly use pointed-eared Pomeranians. A good dog can round up a single stray animal or an entire herd spread out over a large grazing area; it can also be used to keep animals together when its owner is busy or when the whole herd is being driven.

Once he was satisfied that all was well with the reindeer, Johan Henrik scanned the surrounding hillsides through his binoculars for the others. The whole herd was scattered over a large area, and so we moved on to check another group.

At midday on a January day, the moon rises behind Kautokeino Church.

During the polar night, Johan Henrik and his dog keep watch over the herd at their pastures.

There were about 3,000 animals in the herd, but they did not all belong to Johan Henrik. For centuries the Saami have formed work-groups called Sii'das. Although each reindeer is individually owned by a member of the Sii'da, the deer are managed as a joint herd and all the work is shared. Johan Henrik's Sii'da comprised five separate families. Grouping the reindeer together as a herd makes them less vulnerable to attack from predators such as wolverines.

It was almost dark when we pulled up outside a small cabin where we would spend the night. Johan Henrik lit the old wood-burning kitchen range and collected more firewood from a stack outside. Soon the stove was roaring and the cabin gradually warmed up. We made coffee and ate dried reindeer meat and bread for our evening meal. Johan Henrik told me that the herd spends every winter in this area. They had been here since the previous November, when they had returned from their summer pastures on the coast. This cabin was one of several in the area that his Sii'da used while they were working with the reindeer.

Before turning in for the night, I went outside. It was beautifully clear and, above all, silent. The full moon reflecting off the snow made it surprisingly light and I could easily see the hills around us in the distance. The place felt a little eerie, but maybe that was because Johan Henrik's brother-in-law, Aslak, had told me that the cabin was haunted. Apparently, some years ago, as he was returning from a nearby hilltop at dusk after checking the herd, he saw a man standing by the cabin with a reindeer sled. He was pleased, thinking he would have company for the night; but when he reached the cabin there was no sign of the man or the reindeer sled. Mysteriously, neither were there any tracks to be seen in the snow.

I was woken early the next morning by Johan Henrik moving around the cabin. A pot of strong coffee was already steaming on the range. The weather was good, and after a quick breakfast we packed up and went to check on more of the herd. Around noon, we began to head back to Kautokeino. On the way we met Aslak, who was on his way out to the herd. The Sii'da operates an informal rota among the men, who take it in turns to keep watch over the herd.

Back at his home in Kautokeino, Johan relaxed in a leather armchair in his living room, while his wife, Berit, brought us coffee and cake. The house was comfortable and simply furnished. In common with many Norwegian homes it had a television and a kitchen equipped with microwave and magimix. Many of the Saami reindeer-herding families in Norway today enjoy a relatively high standard of living.

Towards the end of March the reindeer were near Badasjokka. It was time to gather them together so that they could be counted. The herders also use this opportunity to sort and separate any strays that have got among them from other herds. Most of the members of the Johan Henrik's Sii'da went to Badasjokka to help. They had a camp there, which consisted of a couple of cabins and a large wooden corral.

In a hut at Badasjokka, Johan Henrik warms up in front of the stove after a day's work.

In the early morning the men left the camp on their snowmobiles to gather up the herd. It was several hours before they returned. I could hear them coming from quite far away. The silence of this Arctic wilderness was broken by the drone of the snowmobiles, the clanking of the bells on the reindeer, the shouts of the herders and the yapping of the dogs as they rounded up the stragglers.

Once the reindeer were in the corral, men, women and teenage children all grabbed lassos; walking slowly among the reindeer, they singled out animals to catch. Every so often a lasso would be thrown and a struggle would ensue as one of the

LEFT Carrying an antler and a lasso, Berit walks across a reindeer corral at Badasjokka.

RIGHT Berit walks among the reindeer at their winter pastures near Badasjokka.

OVERLEAF Nils Johan uses a length of hessian to help him drive reindeer into a corral.

herders fought to subdue a reindeer. Most of the time the reindeer just calmly walked round and round the corral in an anti-clockwise direction. Why Finnmark's reindeer always walk anti-clockwise in a corral nobody seems to know. The Saami just accept it, saying that the reindeer 'follow the sun'.

In the afternoon, members of a neighbouring Sii'da arrived to reclaim some of their reindeer that had become mixed with Johan Henrik's herd. Many reindeer look alike, but the Saami are always able to tell who owns a particular animal by its ear-markings. Each owner has their own unique reindeer mark, usually received as a child when given their first reindeer. The marks consist of a combination of nicks cut into one of the animal's ears with a knife. Each family has its own way of arranging a particular selection of nicks to form the family mark. These marks have to be registered with the Reindeer Herders Administration, and this ensures that different herders don't use the same mark and that any ownership dispute can be easily settled.

At a christening, a Saami woman tends a baby in a traditional komsa *(cradle).*

As the day wore on, more and more of the reindeer were released from the corral once they were no longer needed. Johan Henrik and the other herders worked late into evening. Once the sun had set, it became bitterly cold, but there was still plenty of twilight to work by. Johan Henrik and Berit were looking for reindeer that still had some back-fat left on them after the winter; these were the ones that would be good to eat. They had invited 200 guests to attend the wedding of their eldest daughter at Kautokeino in two weeks' time, and they needed to kill 15 of their reindeer in order to feed everyone.

Whenever they caught a suitable animal, Johan Henrik wrestled it to the ground and pinned it down on its back. Then, taking his knife from its sheath, he plunged it first into the reindeer's heart and then into the spine at the base of its neck. The animal died in a matter of seconds.

Easter has always been a traditional time for the Saami to gather at Kautokeino. It was often the last opportunity that many of the reindeer herders had to see their friends and relatives before they left on the spring migration to the coast. Easter at Kautokeino is a very social occasion and various events, such as reindeer-racing, are held there. It is also a time when marriages often take place.

In Norway, the Saami abandoned their own animistic religious beliefs a long time ago. Most were converted to the Lutheran faith, and marriages nowadays take place in the wooden church at Kautokeino.

Although some Saami marry young, many prefer to wait, and some already have several children before finally taking the plunge. The daughter of Johan Henrik and Berit, Ellen Margarete, was 26 years old, and her fiancé was a reindeer-herder.

Although she worked as a teacher, she owned her own reindeer, which she had accumulated since she was a child. Her father and brother look after them for her, but eventually she will have to give all her reindeer to her husband as a dowry.

On her wedding day, Ellen Margarete looked resplendent in her traditional clothing in a combination of bright red and dark blue, adorned with striking silver and gold jewellery. After the ceremony, family and friends gathered outside the simple wooden church. Their bright national costumes added a mass of colour to an otherwise dull day.

Kautokeino is a sprawling village of 2,000 people. With its Best Western Hotel, a video-rental store and two supermarkets, it looks like many of the other small communities in northern Norway. There is nothing about the buildings that gives the impression of being distinctly Saami. This is largely due to the fact that, during the Second World War, the retreating German army 'torched' most of Finnmark, so there is little left of the original Saami communities. When villages like Kautokeino were rebuilt after the war, Norwegian-style wooden houses with interiors of stripped pine were constructed.

The marriage of Ellen Margarete to Aslak Skum at Kautokeino Church.

Kautokeino has always been a stronghold of Saami culture. Today, it has its own Saami college and cultural centre. The Saami who live in the Kautokeino area are among the most traditional to be found in Lapland, and many still wear their brightly coloured national costume on a daily basis.

The association between the Saami and reindeer is so strong that it has given rise to the popular misconception that all Saami herd reindeer. In fact, nowadays, less than 8 per cent of the Saami work with reindeer. This is largely because there is a limited amount of suitable reindeer pastures in Finnmark and these are already grazed to capacity. Reindeer-herding is nevertheless still a fairly major operation, with some 450 families tending upwards of 147,000 animals in an area about the size of Denmark.

Each spring, some internal trigger prompts the reindeer to begin the journey towards their summer pastures at the coast. At the end of April, Johan Henrik's herd had begun to move slowly northwest from Badasjokka.

For Johan Henrik and the other members of the Sii'da, the long journey to the coast began by corralling the herd again and then segregating the 2,000 pregnant females away from the males and yearlings. Four members of the Sii'da left almost immediately with the females, so they could reach their summer pastures before calving began.

On 30 April I went by snowmobile with Johan Henrik to Vuorasvarre where the remainder of the herd were grazing. Six other members of the Sii'da joined us there, as we also prepared to leave for the coast. All were relatives of Johan Henrik, and included his youngest daughter, two brothers-in-law, and three nephews. In earlier times, Saami women would accompany their menfolk on the migration with their young children. Nowadays, most of them drive directly to the summer pastures by car. It is not difficult to see why. Many have grown used to modern comforts and are reluctant to endure a ten-day trek across the tundra when they can drive to the coast in a few hours by road.

After rounding up the animals, one of the dominant males was lassoed and fastened to a snowmobile, which was driven slowly in front to lead the way. The rest of the herd followed behind, and five snowmobiles, 11 sleds and three dogs brought up the rear and encouraged stragglers to keep up.

We headed northwest, descending through scattered birch forest into the Kautokeino river valley. After crossing the frozen river, we began to climb again up onto the vast expanse of open tundra that is called *vidda* in North Norway. We had 150 miles of tundra ahead of us without a single road to cross before we neared the coast. The route we would be taking to the herd's summer pastures on the Island of Arnoy had been used by members of the Sii'da and their ancestors since 1833.

It was a beautiful, bright and sunny day, but despite the good conditions the herd pushed along at barely 1 mile per hour. Johan Henrik had told me that many of last year's calves were 'sick'. Already, some 200 of the weakest had been trucked to the

Traditional Saami man's dress worn in the Kautokeino area.

Aslak carries an exhausted young reindeer on his snowmobile during the spring migration to the coast.

summer pastures by road. The soft snow and the arduousness of the terrain quickly tired the reindeer. Twelve calves collapsed, exhausted, and had to be loaded onto sleds and taken back to Kautokeino so they could be transported by road.

In the late afternoon, we stopped for a break. We made coffee and ate some dried reindeer meat and fresh bread that Johan Henrik's wife had baked for the journey. Then we set off again, with Johan Henrik leading the way across the tundra on a pair of heavy wooden skis.

At midnight, Johan Henrik reached the top of a hill; he stopped and slipped off his skis. The sun had sunk beneath the horizon an hour earlier, but the glow of the Arctic twilight still bathed the tundra in soft shades of blue. Scraping at the snow with his skin boot, Johan Henrik uncovered some lichens; there would be enough food for his animals. Behind him, the 1,000 reindeer trudged wearily through the snow, following his tracks in a meandering file stretching back for almost a mile.

The reindeer began to spread out over the surrounding area to graze, while Johan Henrik looked for a suitable place to make camp. The spot he selected was on a ridge and exposed to wind from every direction, but it was high enough to keep watch on the reindeer herd. When the others arrived the draft reindeer were unharnessed, the sleds unpacked and a *lavo*, a traditional teepee-style tent, was erected with birch twigs as a floor and reindeer skins laid over them. It was not long before a pot of snow sizzled above a blazing fire in the centre of the tent. Inge Anna, Johan Henrik's daughter, prepared a meal of fried reindeer meat and bread, washed down with strong coffee. She normally works as a loans officer at the bank in Kautokeino, but had taken some leave so she could come along to help her father. The migration offered her an opportunity to keep in touch with her Saami roots. As the night wore on, herders and dogs sprawled on the reindeer skins to sleep. Only Aslak, one of Johan Henrik's brothers-in-law, stayed awake. It was his turn to keep watch over the herd.

It was freezing cold in the tent when I awoke the following morning. The fire had died down to a few embers. Aslak collected some wood from one of the sleds and soon had the fire blazing again. He made coffee, so strong that you could have stood a spoon upright in it, but that seems to be the way that most Saami herders like it. For breakfast we roasted chunks of reindeer meat on sticks over the open fire, and afterwards we prepared for another day's travelling. Johan Henrik put a fresh lining of dried sedge grass into his curly-toed reindeer-skin boots. The grass not only makes them comfortable to walk in but also offers excellent insulation against the cold.

By 10 am we were on the move again. It was another fine day. The sun shone strong and warm, and once again the soft snow took its toll of the herd. About 50 weak calves slowed us down, and 18 ended up being transported on sleds. Later one of Aslak's calves died; it was to be the first of many. Over the next few days, we made slow progress, because of the numbers of exhausted animals.

Travelling on skis, Johan Henrik walks in front of the the herd on the spring migration.

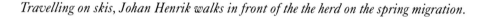

When we camped in the evenings the mood among the herders was subdued. Things were not going well with the animals. Things have not been going well for reindeer anywhere in northern Norway for a good number of years. Up until the 1960s, reindeer-herding in Norway was a form of subsistence pastoralism – a harsh but free way of life with a rich tradition. Since then, it has become increasingly intensive. An agreement between the Saami herders and the government-operated Reindeer Herders Administration resulted in herders benefitting from generous subsidies. This transformed reindeer-herding into an attractive financial proposition.

LEFT A *Saami* lavo *(tent) at dusk at a herders' camp on the spring migration.*

OPPOSITE Johan Logje stuffs *his reindeer-skin boots with Arctic grass to keep his feet warm.*

The numbers of reindeer in Finnmark steadily increased until there were far too many for the pastures available in Finnmark. There were two main reasons for this. Firstly, too many herders were trying to match the high Norwegian standard of living from an activity that had only ever provided a subsistence lifestyle. Secondly, there were too few alternative employment possibilities for young Saami; therefore many felt they had no option but to turn to the traditional pursuit of reindeer-herding.

The overcrowding of pastures has resulted in many of the reindeer becoming emaciated and weak, not just from the shortage of food but also from the increasing infestation of parasites. In 1993, the average slaughter weight of a six-month-old reindeer calf from the Kautokeino area was a mere 37 pounds. A healthy animal of that age should weigh between 65 and 90 pounds. When I showed some photographs of reindeer in Finnmark to a Siberian reindeer-herder, he told me he thought they looked like dogs. That may sound a bit far-fetched, but my own dog, an English Springer Spaniel, weighs 39 pounds.

Reindeer-herding has become far less labour-intensive in recent years, with the widespread use of fences to prevent animals straying and mixing with other herds. It has also become considerably more mechanized with snowmobiles, motorboats, four-wheelers ('quad bikes'), airplanes and even helicopters being used to herd the reindeer. These 'improvements' may have made life easier for the herders, but they have not benefitted the reindeer. Modern mechanized methods of herding are also responsible for causing a lot of stress to the reindeer. One veterinary surgeon, who inspected meat at the slaughter-house in Kautokeino, told me how he had made a random inspection of the carcasses slaughtered from one herd after the autumn migration. Seventy per cent of the animals he examined had fresh stomach ulcers.

How many reindeer there are in Finnmark remains something of a mystery. The official figure in 1994 was 147,000, though one government official told me he thought it was probably nearer 200,000. The difficulty of ascertaining an accurate census of the reindeer population is that the figures are supplied by the herders themselves.

In the past, the Saami were taxed on the number of reindeer they owned. Asking a herder how many reindeer he had was akin to asking someone how much money they

A Saami reindeer herders' camp at sunset on the spring migration.

had in their bank account. The Saami, like most people in this world, do not relish paying taxes, so many deliberately concealed the true number of reindeer they owned. This resulted in what became known as the 'hidden herds'. Although the system of taxation changed in 1985, many Saami still deeply mistrust the Norwegian authorities, and are often reluctant to cooperate with government officials.

Under Norwegian law, only the Saami are permitted to keep reindeer. Reindeer-herding plays two roles in Norway. Firstly, it underpins the Saami culture and without it the culture would disintegrate. Its second role is meat-production. Each autumn the herders slaughter about 20–25 per cent of their animals and most of the meat is sent to southern Norway. There it is expensive and viewed as a luxury. It represents only 1 per cent of the total meat consumed in Norway – the equivalent of one meal of reindeer meat per year for each member of the population.

How the current problem of too many reindeer will be solved remains to be seen. It seems unlikely that the Norwegian government will take the tough action necessary to bring about the significant reduction in the reindeer population. As one Finnmark resident explained, 'the government treated the Saami very badly in the past and they are now frightened of being seen to act against them'.

Some people I spoke to in Finnmark, like the Saami vet, Hurdis Gaup, believe that correcting the situation will be left to nature. 'A bad winter might sort the problem,' she told me. 'If the reindeer lichen become iced over in the early spring, many thousands of reindeer will starve to death because they won't have the necessary energy reserves.'

Johan Henrik knows only too well how devastating a major die-off can be for reindeer-herders. During the hard winter of 1968, his Sii'da lost 1,200 of their 2,000 animals.

On the evening of our fifth day on the migration, we made camp at a beautiful spot by the side of a small ravine on the Troms/Finnmark border. After we had eaten, Inge Anna suggested we watch the *Eurovision Song Contest* on television. I thought for a minute that she must be joking; we were in about as wild and remote a place that it is possible to be in Norway, and I guessed that we were at least 60 miles from the nearest television set. As it turned out, I was wrong. There was a small hut that belonged to another Sii'da only a few miles away. Although the *Eurovision Song Contest* is not exactly a programme I would normally go out of my way to watch, I joined Inge Anna and her two cousins Nils Peter and Mikkel, who took two of the snowmobiles and drove to the hut. There, we were welcomed by Anders Eira. The hut was small but, considering its location, remarkably well equipped with a generator, colour television and mobile 'phone. Anders made us all coffee while we settled down for an evening of television.

The next morning I was awake much earlier than I would have liked. The persistent croaking calls of a ptarmigan, that sounded like it was just a few inches from my head, made it impossible for me to sleep on. Before we continued our journey towards the coast, Johan Henrik attempted to catch three fresh reindeer to pull his

sleds. With his lasso at the ready he walked among the herd, looking for replacements. In a matter of a few minutes he had lassoed and harnessed two strong geldings; the third, however, was a different story. It was a highly spirited animal, and, with the rest of the Sii'da looking on, he battled with it for half an hour. Finally, jubilant and sweating, he was able to subdue and harness it.

The weather was overcast and for much of the day our journey took us along the Finnish border which was marked by a fence partially covered by drifting snow. That night we had the relative luxury of using a small wooden cabin that was just on the Norwegian side of the border. After our evening meal, Aslak passed round a bottle of homebrew. He told me it was veterinary alcohol. I believed him – it certainly had a kick like a horse. Afterwards we played cards, before we sprawled out on reindeer skins on the floor to sleep.

When I awoke the next morning, a strong wind howled outside the cabin; blowing snow had reduced the visibility down to a few yards. It became a welcome day of rest for the reindeer as well as the herders, who spent most of the time relaxing in the hut drinking coffee and playing cards. In the evening Johan Henrik boiled up a large saucepan of reindeer meat and some leg bones, which he split open with a knife, and we ate the marrow.

By the following morning, the weather had improved and we prepared to move again. Skiing with a distinctive rolling gait, Johan Henrik set off in front of the herd, leading a train of three heavily laden reindeer sleds. The journey began with a long climb up a mountainside. Although it was colder and the snow firmer, the ascent proved too tiring for some of the calves. Several collapsed and we had to leave them behind. We were already carrying as many exhausted calves as we could, and there was no more room on the sleds. The terrain was becoming much more undulating now, an indication that we were already nearing the coast.

Fortunately, it was a short move to the next lichen pasture and we reached it soon after midday. Once we had finished putting up the *lavos*, Mikkel and Nils Peter took off on one of the snowmobiles to go to a nearby lake where they wanted to jig for Arctic char through the ice. Our camp was close to Seittikielas, a mountain where there was a *seide*, a stone idol. In earlier times, the Saami used to leave offerings of meat and money there, believing that it would bring them good luck.

In the middle of the afternoon, I was sitting in brilliant sunshine enjoying the spectacular view of the surrounding hills, when the fog began to roll in. Within a matter of minutes the visibility was reduced to less than 50 yards. I began to wonder whether Mikkel and Nils Peter would have difficulty finding their way back to our camp. The Saami are used to travelling in these kind of adverse weather conditions, and at 6 pm, they returned safely with a bag full of Arctic char that they had caught. Aslak cleaned

LEFT Johan Henrik harnesses one of the reindeer that will pull a sled on the migration.

OVERLEAF At dawn, the reindeer begin their descent of the Kildal Valley towards the coast.

A reindeer swimming the channel between the mainland and the island of Kagen.

and poached some of the fish over the fire, and they tasted delicious. It turned into an exquisitely beautiful evening; golden sunshine bathed the high ground, while fog still hung in the valley.

On the tenth day, we began the descent towards the coast. It was much warmer now, and there was the sound of squelching as the reindeer trudged through the soft wet snow. Patches of snow-free ground became more frequent and the reindeer calves stopped to graze wherever they could. I heard foxes calling to each other across the valley. It was at least reassuring to know that nature would soon clear up the trail of dead reindeer calves we had left behind on the tundra. We made slow progress, travelling behind a group of 200 of the weaker calves. In the early afternoon we made camp again. Johan Henrik explained that from now on we would travel at night when it was colder and the snow firmer, which would make it easier for the reindeer.

On the 11th evening we prepared to move again. We packed the sleds and set off at 10 pm. The weather was clear and cold and the snow much firmer. We had a steep ascent up to a mountain pass ahead of us, but soon after we set off we ran into problems, as some of the herd scattered. Johan Henrik and the other members of the Sii'da had difficulty keeping the animals together. Apparently, the problem was that there was a strong southerly wind and we were heading north. Aslak explained that reindeer don't like travelling with the wind. Left to their own devices, they will always travel against it. 'Sometimes when it is calm,' Aslak told me, 'the reindeer will begin to move in the direction the wind will come from 24 hours before it actually blows.'

By 2 am in the morning we reached the last mountain pass. The 1,000 reindeer were dwarfed by the high mountains all around as the herd began the final descent towards the coast, following the route of the frozen Kildal River. We continued our journey right through the night. The terrain was demanding; at times the animals floundered in deep drifts of soft snow and splashed through foot-deep water on top of the frozen river.

By morning, they had spread out onto the surrounding hillsides to graze on reindeer moss. A downpour signalled that we had almost reached the coast. The reindeer would rest for a few days, and then when the weather had improved Johan Henrik and the other members of the Sii'da would swim them across the 500-yard channel to the island of Kagen, and later to their summer pastures on the island of Arnoy.

My time in Finnmark was over. I hitched a ride to Skjervoy and then caught the coast boat south to Bergen. During the voyage, I had time to reflect on the problems faced by the Johan Henrik and the other herders. Would they manage to solve the overcrowding of their pastures and the numbers of sick and starving reindeer? I reasoned that a people as resilient as the Saami who had been able to maintain an ancient herding culture in mainland Europe into the 1990s could probably solve almost any problem they wanted to.

Johan Logje warms himself by the fire in his tent during the spring migration.

The Inuit of the Canadian Eastern Arctic
Out on the Land

There are about 34,000 Inuit in the Canadian North today. Most of them live in the Northwest Territories – a vast and seemingly empty wilderness that encompasses about one-third of the land area of the whole of Canada. In the northeast of this region, in Foxe Basin, lies the small island of Igloolik ('place of houses'). This low-lying island, comprised largely of shattered limestone, is situated some 300 miles north of the Arctic Circle. It has the kind of severe climate that is typical of the high Arctic. In winter the temperature can drop to around -62°F (-52°C) and only averages 43°F (6°C) in July. The surrounding seas are only ice-free for a brief ten weeks each year, and during the winter the sun does not appear above the horizon for two months.

This northern part of Foxe Basin has been occupied by the Inuit and their ancestors for at least 4,000 years. In former times, their whole life was dominated by the need to hunt game. They depended largely on seals, which they hunted at breathing-holes and the floe edge, as well as other sea mammals such as walrus, belugas and narwhals. Inland, they hunted caribou, trapped foxes and fished the rivers and lakes for Arctic char.

ABOVE *Children of the Taqqaugaq family warmly dressed in caribou-skin clothing.*

LEFT *Frost-smoke rises off the open sea as Louis Tapardjuk walks along the floe edge.*

Although the Igloolik area was first visited by white men in the early 1820s, when British explorers Captains William Parry and George Lyon arrived in their ships, the *Fury* and the *Hecla*, it was not until the late 1930s, with the arrival of the missionaries and traders, that a Hudson's Bay Company trading-post was established there and Igloolik began to change dramatically.

LEFT Kigutikaarjuk and his wife Annie discuss their purchases at the store in Igloolik.

OPPOSITE During a recess, schoolchildren play outside the school in Igloolik.

The opening of a DEW (distant early warning) line station 45 miles south at Hall Beach brought improved communications, and soon Igloolik became a government administration centre with its own school, nursing station and RCMP (Royal Canadian Mounted Police) detachment. Gradually the Iglulingmiut – as the Inuit of this area are called – left their remote camps for a more sedentary existence 'in town'. Today, only a handful of families still spend the whole year out on the land, while the settlement itself has grown into a community of 1,200. Like many other northern native settlements, Igloolik consists of rows of bungalows, the building materials for which are transported up from the south each summer on the 'sealift'.

In Igloolik nowadays, you will find an fascinating mixture of traditional Inuit culture contrasting with the modern world of the *qallunaaq* ('white man'). Snowmobiles, the modern form of Arctic winter transport, speed along the same trails as dogsleds; in Inuit homes, fashionable skiwear hangs up alongside traditional caribou-skin clothing. Igloolik has its own small radio station that broadcasts news, music and messages in Inuktitut throughout the day. Televisions and VCRs are to be found in almost every home and the local stores stock the same videos that can be found the world over.

Despite the fact that Igloolik's stores are stacked with an impressive display of TV dinners', hamburgers, cookies, fizzy drinks and other junk foods, most Inuit still rely on traditional staple 'land foods', such as caribou, seal, walrus and Arctic char.

Although there are only about 40 full-time hunters in Igloolik these days, practically everybody hunts on a part-time basis. Hunting is still very important to the Iglulingmiut, not only because of the value of the food it provides but also because it is the basis of Inuit culture.

By 1999, the Iglulingmiut will be among the 22,600 Inuit from the eastern Northwest Territories who will benefit from the Nunavut ('our land') landclaim. Under this claim, the Inuit will receive a total of $1.4 billion paid over 14 years as well as title to 135,000 square miles of land. Other benefits include wildlife harvesting rights and participation on wildlife and other resource management boards within the territory.

. . . .

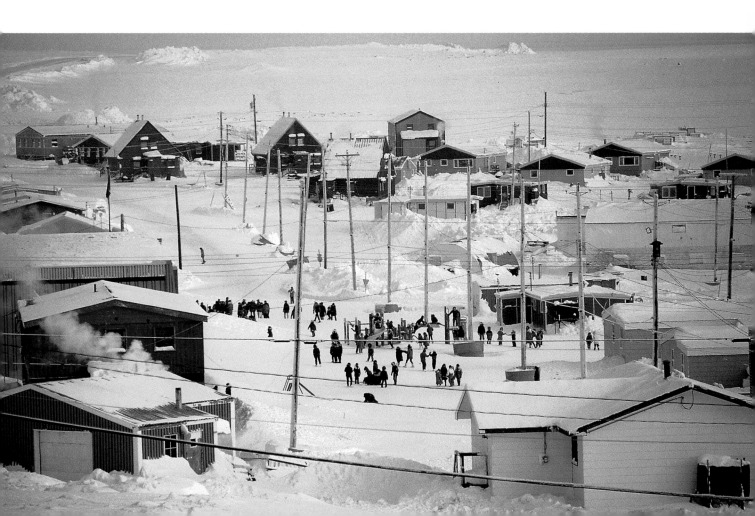

I sat on the sled behind Kangok's snowmobile as he drove flat out across the sea-ice of Foxe Basin. With only a caribou skin between me and the wooden sled it was an uncomfortable ride. The snow on the sea-ice had been packed down hard by the wind. In some places there was no snow at all to cushion the ride; the ice was shiny and slick and the sled snaked from side to side. I clung on to the lashings of the sled and attempted to shield my face from the snow and ice kicked up by the snowmobile. I was dressed from head to foot in traditional caribou-skin clothing and, although the temperature was well below -22°F (-30°C), I felt comfortably warm.

We had left the community of Igloolik an hour before, and were heading northeast towards Baffin Island. I was planning to visit the Taqqaugaqs' family outpost camp at Iglurjuat ('the place of large houses') on the west side of Steensby Inlet. Kangok and his travelling companion Akumalik were going wolf-hunting further down the coast, and had agreed to drop me off on their way.

After a few hours, we reached the narrow channel that separates Jens Munk Island from Baffin. A strong current ensures that the channel never freezes over completely, and a curtain of frost-smoke hung over the open water. We stopped for a welcome break; Kangok lit his Coleman stove and put on a pan of snow to make tea. A seal surfaced in the open water and both Kangok and Akumalik grabbed their rifles and ran closer to the edge of the ice. Areas of water that remain unfrozen throughout the Arctic winter, called

Nutarariaq out hunting on a skidoo in the winter near Igloolik.

Nutarariaq collecting snow to make tea on a hunting-trip.

polynyas, have always been good hunting-places for the Inuit. Kangok and Akumalik waited for a while, but the seal didn't surface again and they returned to the task of making tea.

After drinking a mug of hot tea and eating some pilot biscuits, Kangok and Akumalik refuelled their snowmobiles. Then we set off again across the sea-ice, heading out into Murray Maxwell Bay. After nine hours of sitting on the sled, I was relieved when Kangok finally brought his snowmobile to a halt and announced that we had arrived at Iglurjuat. To begin with, I thought he must be joking, because I couldn't see any sign of a building – the large wooden hut there was completely covered by the winter's snow. If it had not been for some oildrums, a tethered dog-team and a couple of snowmobiles, you would never have known that this was an outpost camp.

Two young children emerged from the hut, curious to see who had arrived. They were followed moments later by Theresia Taqqaugaq, who invited us back to the hut. We followed Theresia down several steps, cut in the snow, that led to the door. It was dim inside, the only light coming from a single window located above the door. As my eyes adjusted to the light I was surprised by the number of people inside. Theresia told me that, altogether, there were 14 members of her family living there: five adults and nine children. With the exception of one grown-up son who worked in the mine at Nanisivik on Baffin Island, all her children were at the camp. Her husband Augustine was out hunting with their son Luke, but they would be back later.

It was warm inside. I struggled out of my caribou-skin clothing and gradually thawed out over a mug of hot tea and bannock. The hut was quite large, about 25 feet square, and comprised just a single room heated by an oil-stove. After finishing their tea, Kangok and Akumalik prepared to leave, and I thanked them for the ride.

Augustine returned from seal-hunting at sunset with Luke. They had not had any success. As darkness closed in, Theresia lit two kerosene pressure lamps and began to prepare an evening meal of boiled Arctic char for the family. Afterwards, we talked for a while, mainly about hunting. Recently, they had been hunting seal and caribou. The caribou had been plentiful this winter and Augustine had also shot a polar bear. In a few weeks he planned to travel up north, to fish for Arctic char near Mary River. I was very tired after my long and bumpy ride from Igloolik and climbed into my sleeping-bag to sleep.

RIGHT Children asleep at the Taqqaugaqs' outpost camp at Iglurjuat.

OPPOSITE The Taqqaugaq family pose in front of their outpost camp at Iglurjuat on Baffin Island.

The next day was sunny and cold, with no wind. Augustine and Theresia were up early making tea and fresh bannock, while everyone else slept on. Around midday, Augustine prepared to go caribou-hunting, and asked me if I wanted to join him. Although I still ached from the previous day's long journey, I jumped at the opportunity. It only takes an Inuk a few minutes to prepare for a day's hunting. I always need a lot longer. I sorted my camera gear and put on my fur clothing as quickly as I could. I was anxious not to delay Augustine who was already outside refuelling his snowmobile. Once he had lashed his rifle and hunting-gear onto the sled, he started the snowmobile and we set off inland. The surface of the snow, covering the tundra, had been sculpted into a series of unending ridges by the wind. It was mostly flat, but whenever we came to a small hill Augustine would stop and scan the surrounding landscape through his binoculars for caribou.

Augustine prepares to skin a caribou he has just shot on Baffin Island.

We travelled for several hours but there was no sign of any caribou. I had just about given up on finding any, when from the top of a small hill we spotted a group of five animals in the distance. Augustine drove the snowmobile very slowly towards them and after a while he cut the engine and began to approach them cautiously on foot. The wind was in his favour; the caribou had not seen us and they continued to graze. Whenever one of them looked up, Augustine would stop and remain motionless until it carried on eating; then he would continue. When Augustine was a little over 150 yards away, the caribou seemed to sense danger. They stopped grazing, raised their heads and scented the air uneasily. Augustine was lying prostrate on the ground as he aimed his battered rifle. He squeezed the trigger; a shot rang out, and the caribou began to run. Suddenly one faltered and then fell to the ground dead.

Augustine stood up and brushed the snow from his caribou-fur clothing as he walked back to the snowmobile, smiling broadly. By the time we reached the caribou, what little blood had spilt onto the snow was already frozen.

Taking a knife from the sled, Augustine set about skinning the caribou, a task he performed with remarkable speed. Within 15 minutes he had folded the skin and loaded the carcass onto the sled. The wind had picked up, and blowing snow was snaking across the tundra. Augustine pointed to narrow clouds near the horizon. 'Maybe later there will be wind,' he said, as once again he pulled the starter-cord of his snowmobile. After checking that I was firmly seated on the sled, he set off back to camp.

To describe the Taqqaugaqs' camp at Iglurjuat as remote would be an understatement. The nearest shop is in Igloolik, 125 miles away. That doesn't seem to worry Augustine or Theresia. Iglurjuat is their winter home and has been since 1983 when, disillusioned with settlement life in Igloolik, they took their children out of school and returned to a more traditional life out on the land.

The sound of our return brought Theresia and several of the children out of the hut, all curious to see how we had fared on the hunt. The caribou carcass was taken from the sled and put up on a meat rack, well out of the reach of the dogs.

Back inside the hut, Theresia prepared a meal for the whole family, placing walrus meat, a caribou haunch, and an Arctic char, all raw, on a plastic sheet on the floor. We all gathered round to eat, hacking off pieces of meat and fat with a knife. Theresia's homemade bannock and some cookies were among the few concessions to white man's food.

Augustine's prediction of bad weather proved correct. We had barely finished eating when the plastic sheeting stretched across the hut's small window began to flap violently as the wind increased. Within a matter of minutes, blowing snow cut the visibility down to 25 yards. As darkness fell, Augustine called Igloolik and another outpost camp on his transceiver, his only link with the outside world. It was windy there too; it seemed that the bad weather was widespread.

We spent the evening chatting and playing cards for matches. Luke must have won enough matches to keep his Coleman stove lit for the next year. As the evening drew on, one by one the family stretched out on the communal sleeping platform. As we settled down for the night, the hut became quiet; I was very aware of the howling wind outside and grateful for the warmth of the hut. 'Maybe there will be fine weather tomorrow,' said Augustine, as he turned off the kerosene pressure lamp.

This time, Augustine's weather prediction proved over-optimistic. The storm was still raging the next day, confining us to the hut, with only an occasional brief excursion outside to feed the dogs or collect ice. Everyone kept busy, and the hut was transformed into a workshop. Luke stripped down one of the snowmobile engines on the floor; Theresia cut pieces of sealskin for a pair of *kamik* (boots) for her grandson; and their two teenage daughters spent most of the time entertaining the younger children or thumbing through magazines while listening to popular music on a Walkman.

Augustine began work on a soapstone carving, chipping away at the stone, first with a hatchet and later with a pocket knife, as he gradually transformed the stone into the shape of a walrus. Augustine is a talented carver and in periods of bad weather or when the hunting is lean he makes soapstone carvings which he sells to the cooperative store in Igloolik. From the proceeds he is able to buy supplies of food and hunting equipment. Augustine told me that, from the sale of three carvings the previous summer, he had been able to buy a new outboard motor for his boat. The sale of skins, mainly fox and wolf, also helps to finance Augustine's life as a hunter.

OVERLEAF *An Inuk and his dog-team sledge across the ice of Foxe Basin during a winter storm.*

133

Aakuainuk drives his dog-team through tidal ice near Igloolik.

The nine children at the camp ranged from Augustine and Theresia's two-year-old grandson, Leonard, to their sixteen-year-old son, Marc. Theresia has no regrets about taking her children out of school. 'They learn more useful things with us out on the land,' she explained. She herself plays many roles, including hunter's wife, mother, teacher and priest, for the family are Catholics and she holds a service at the camp each Sunday. She also acts as midwife, and delivered her two grandchildren, who were both born at the camp.

One morning we awoke to find three caribou grazing only 100 yards from the hut. Surprisingly, nobody made any attempt to shoot them; this was because, as Luke explained, we already had plenty of caribou meat.

Later, Luke decided to test the snowmobile engine he had been working on by going to a lead in the sea-ice to hunt seals. Many Inuit hunters are able and extremely resourceful mechanics. With the minimum of tools, and often having to improvise for replacement parts, they manage to fix most snowmobile breakdowns. On one cold winter hunting-trip I made with Augustine, the engine of his snowmobile kept cutting out. After lifting back the engine cover, Augustine quickly deduced that the problem was that the carburettor was too cold; he solved the problem by urinating on the carburettor to warm it. This, I later discovered, was common procedure in the Arctic for solving this problem.

Though it is true to say that the snowmobile has largely replaced the dogsled in the Canadian North, in recent years the high cost of buying and operating a snowmobile has resulted in dog-teams making a modest comeback. They may be slower, but they don't break down; they renew themselves and they run on meat, not gasoline. They also have the advantage that, if you are unfortunate enough to get stranded out on the tundra somewhere, you can always eat your dogs to survive. Augustine seemed to have the best of both worlds. He runs a snowmobile and a team of 17 huskies.

When I was out hunting alone with Augustine, communication was a problem at times, as we understood very little of each other's languages. The people of Igloolik speak Inuktitut, the language of the Inuit that is spoken right across the Canadian North, although there are many regional dialects.

For most outsiders, Inuktitut is a difficult language to master. Many of the words sound and look similar, but have very different meanings. This has led to some amusing mistakes. On one occasion an Anglican Minister in the community of Arctic Bay caused much amusement when, during his Sunday sermon, he urged the congregation to 'study their bibles'. The Inuktitut word for a bible is *ijjujut*, but he used the word *igjujuk* by mistake; thus urging them instead to 'study their testicles'!

At dusk Tatigat pulls aside the snow-brick at the entrance to his igloo.

Though they spend most of the year at Iglurjuat, in the spring the family moves to another camp at Ikpik Bay, a good place to hunt seals. Then, later in the early summer, they move again to another camp to fish for Arctic char.

Some of the sites of hunting-camps like Iglurjuat have been used by the Inuit and their ancestors for up to 4,000 years. Before the days of settlement living, camps were scattered right across the Arctic. Each community of Inuit evolved its own seasonal cycle of life, which was dictated both by the needs of the hunters and by the movements of the animals they depended on.

Many of today's settlements in the Canadian North began with just a trading-post back in the pioneering days of the world-famous Hudson's Bay Company. It was its role as the first trading company to establish itself in Arctic Canada that gave rise to the joke that the company's initials stood for 'Here Before Christ'. In those days it was acceptable in southern countries to kill animals for their fur, and traders were eager for the quality skins that the Inuit could provide.

The influence of these early traders had a pronounced effect on the Inuit. They became no longer purely subsistence hunters, but came to depend on trading pelts, particularly those of Arctic foxes, for goods that they quickly came to rely on. Missionaries followed hot on the heels of the traders, and after them came the administrators. Settlements began to be established throughout the North, though many Inuit remained at their hunting-camps.

Hunger and starvation were always an unwelcome part of Inuit life. Even as late as the 1950s, some groups of Inuit were facing starvation. The Canadian government took action and began to pour vast sums of money into the North. Many Inuit were persuaded, and in some cases forced, to abandon their traditional life at hunting-camps for a more sedentary existence in newly formed settlements.

To begin with settlement life must have seemed like paradise for many Inuit – no more starvation, housing in prefabricated bungalows where heat and light came with the flick of a switch, medical care and schooling for their children. Nobody, it seemed, predicted the problems that were to come. Large boarding-schools were built in the major settlements like Churchill, on the coast of Hudson Bay. Inuit children from camps and the smaller communities were sent there to be educated and prepared for life in the modern Arctic. The one thing that the white man had not provided for the Inuit was sufficient employment.

Many young Inuit found themselves trapped between two cultures. Schooling resulted in them spending a considerable time away from their families during their formative years; so, later, they lacked the necessary knowledge and skill to live as hunters. The modern Arctic, however, had little work to offer them, and they were faced with having to live on government handouts. Not surprisingly, their self-esteem plummeted, and in frustration many of them turned to alcohol and drugs; some were driven to suicide.

Aipilik Innuksuk jigging through the ice for cod on a fishing-trip to Ugaqjualik.

By the late 1960s, the Inuit culture seemed to be facing inevitable decline. Some Inuit then realized that living in settlements under the enveloping protective mantle of the government, with television, stores full of costly consumer goods and junk food, was doing more harm than good to their people. It was this realization that led to what was later to become known as the 'back-to-the-land movement', as a growing number of Inuit families, disillusioned with modern settlement living, gave up their homes to move back to hunting-camps.

Tatigat (RIGHT) and his wife Catherine Arnatsiaq (OPPOSITE) photographed at their home in Igloolik.

The government of the Northwest Territories decided to assist those Inuit who wanted to return to the land, and in 1975 it introduced its Outpost Camp Programme. The scheme was later incorporated into what the government called its Community Harvester Assistance Programme, which is operated by the Department of Renewable Resources. It provides both material and financial help to families in the project. 'Basically, what we are doing,' a government official told me, 'is helping people who want to get back onto the land and who otherwise couldn't afford to.'

Tatigat enjoys a moment out on the land near Igloolik.

The Community Harvester Assistance Programme operates in three regions of the Canadian Arctic: Inuvik in the west, Kiktikmeot in the central Arctic, and the Baffin region in the east. Some sites of traditional Inuit camps were in fact never vacated, but many new camps formed as the back-to-the-land movement gathered momentum. There is, of course, a certain irony in the fact that the Canadian government, having spent millions of dollars over two decades to get the Inuit to move off the land and into settlements, is now paying for some of them to move back again. Initially, critics of the scheme saw it as throwing money away on an attempt by some nostalgic members of the Inuit community to turn back the clocks. Admittedly, some Inuit, mainly the young, didn't take to camp life. On the walls of one outpost camp hut I found graffiti that read 'I am so fucken homesick' and 'What a bore!' The young Inuit who became disenchanted with outpost camp life returned to the rock music, videos, satellite television and coffee-bars of the modern Arctic settlements. Some did stay, and new camps were formed as interest in the programme grew. In the early 1970s, before the start of the programme, there were only three Inuit camps left on Baffin Island. By 1986, that figure had increased to 29, and had risen again to 34 by 1995. By then, there was a total of 52 camps in the three regions of the Canadian Arctic where the programme was in operation.

Now, although there are more camps, there are fewer Inuit living out on the land. In the early days of the programme, there were a number of what one Renewable Resources Officer described to me as 'Mega-camps', which had up to 60 Inuit living there at any one time. Nowadays, camps tend to comprise relatively small family groups, and a camp of 15 Inuit would be considered large. There are different reasons for the decline in the numbers of Inuit in camps. Even though unemployment is high in most native settlements, many Inuit still want to belong to the wage-earning community. Most jobs, even if they are just seasonal or part-time, are only to be found in settlements. Also, some Inuit who would prefer to live out on the land don't do so because of family ties. They may have young children at school or elderly relatives that need to be looked after or require medical attention. The family unit is still strong among the Inuit.

In recent years it has become increasingly difficult to earn a cash income as a hunter in the Arctic. Up until the early 1980s, the Inuit were able to rely on selling sealskins to finance their hunting activities. Then, however, they became the innocent victims of campaigns mounted by Greenpeace and other animal-rights groups against Canada's annual harp-seal cull. These campaigns, which were illustrated with gruesome pictures of baby seals being clubbed to death on the ice, brought such a public outcry that the United States government banned all seal-mammal products from its markets. The European Economic Community took similar action, banning the import of all seal products. Inevitably the world market for sealskins collapsed.

During the 1970s, a good-quality sealskin might have fetched Canadian $60 or more at a fur auction. In the spring of 1995 the average price of sealskins at one auction was only $5.68. The collapse of the sealskin market brought economic hardship to

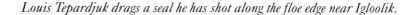

Louis Tepardjuk drags a seal he has shot along the floe edge near Igloolik.

hunting communities throughout the Arctic, and it forced many more native people onto welfare. What seems so unjust is that the Inuit were made to suffer although they had absolutely nothing whatsoever to do with Canada's commercial harp-seal cull. They hunt mainly adult ringed seals, the most common seal found in the Arctic and believed to number in excess of 15 million. They take relatively few harp seals and certainly don't go around clubbing baby 'whitecoats' to death. The Inuit were aggrieved that, before banning sealskins from the world's two major markets, nobody consulted them or took into consideration the importance that seal-hunting plays in their traditional culture. In 1995, the Inuit and other northern peoples were facing the implementation of another European Economic Community fur ban, this time on animals caught by leg-hold traps, such as Arctic fox, another species that Inuit hunters have long depended on for cash. Rosemary Kuptana, one of the Inuit political leaders, compared this new ban to a neutron bomb being dropped on the Inuit: '. . . it leaves the buildings standing and the shell of our people walking around.'

In June 1992, I had the opportunity to spend some time with another outpost-camp family. Niaqutsiaq was about to move with his wife Mary and five children from their winter outpost camp on Baffin Island to a hunting-camp on Jens Munk Island. They had called into Igloolik for supplies and had agreed to take me along with them. We left by snowmobile on a fine summer's evening and headed out across the sea-ice.

At –40°F (–40°C) frost-smoke rises off the open water as hunters gather at the floe edge.

On thin ice, Louis Tepardjuk stands in a floe-edge boat while hunting seals at the ice edge.

Niaqutsiaq's long sled was piled high with supplies and camping equipment. Perched precariously on the top of all of it were his wife and children. I drove behind on another snowmobile. It was the Arctic summer at its most beautiful, calm with clear skies, and, although it was nearly midnight, the sun was still shining. At the floe edge, the sea was like a millpond. Arctic terns swooped and hovered above the open water, and the 'coo-roo-uh' cries from groups of eider ducks in the distance carried across the water. I spotted a snowmobile and the figures of two hunters in the distance. Niaqutsiaq stopped by them. One of them was his nephew, Levi, who was hunting seals with Esau, a young Inuk from Repulse Bay. Five seals and three ducks lay on the ice by their sled.

Hunting seals from the floe edge is a popular form of hunting among the Iglulingmiut. It is something that can be done for most of the year, as, even in the middle of winter, the floe edge is rarely more than an hour's travel from the community by snowmobile. Hunters choose a likely spot along the ice edge and then wait for seals to surface within rifle range. One essential piece of equipment for this type of hunting is a small, wooden flat-bottomed boat that hunters usually carry with them on their sled. After a hunter shoots a seal, he launches the boat from the edge of the ice and paddles out to retrieve the dead animal. During the winter a large layer of blubber ensures that dead seals float, whereas in the summer months the bodies quickly sink.

It was one 1 am as we neared Ikpiugalik ('having a raised beach') on the south side of Jens Munk island. We drove over some tidal cracks and then up onto the land which was still mostly snow-covered. Eventually we came to a halt by a flat area of gravel where the snow had already melted. The whole family helped unpack the sled and put up the white canvas-walled tent. Sheets of plywood were used to make a sleeping platform at one end and caribou skins were laid on top of them. Once the tent was up and all the guy ropes were securely fastened to heavy rocks, Niaqutsiaq set up his transceiver and antenna. It was not long before he was chatting to family and friends in Igloolik.

Transceivers are now widely used by the Inuit when they are at outpost camps or out on hunting-trips. They bring an element of safety into a way of life that is often fraught with danger. The Iglulingmiut gave transceivers the local name of *uvaq*, derived from the English word 'over' that they heard so often during radio transmissions.

By 4 am, I was tired and prepared to crawl into my sleeping-bag. The older children were still on the go, and took off excitedly to explore the area around our camp. In the summer months, when it's light 24 hours a day, and the Inuit are out at camps, they don't sleep and eat at fixed times. They often hunt all night and then sleep in the day.

OPPOSITE *An Inuk woman using her teeth to soften a sealskin.*

BELOW *At his summer camp, Niaqutsiaq chats on the radio to other hunters.*

The following day I woke at noon. Niaqutsiaq was already up rolling a cigarette and drinking coffee. The children were still asleep, tired after being up all night. Our camp had grown while I had slept; there were two more tents nearby. Mary told me that Niaqutsiaq's uncle Ulayuruluk, his wife Sarah, his son Lot and his two grandchildren had arrived early that morning.

It was a beautiful day again and I decided to go for a walk. Summer was certainly beginning. On the snow-free areas of tundra, purple saxifrage was already starting to flower and some of the dwarf willow was in bud. From the higher ground behind our camp, I scanned the ice through my binoculars. There were several seals basking on the ice beside a lead; later, Niaqutsiaq went out and managed to shoot one of them.

The size of our camp increased steadily. First Levi and Esau arrived. Then, during the course of the evening, they were followed by several families who had left Igloolik for a weekend out on the land. On

a fine Friday, after the offices and stores have closed, a steady stream of snowmobiles can often be seen leaving Igloolik, in much the same way as cars can be seen leaving any southern town as people head off for a weekend in the country.

Hunters head for Ikpiugalik because it is a good place to hunt seals at this time of year. It is a very social type of hunting that can involve the whole family. During the spring, seals widen their breathing-holes by clawing at the ice until the hole is wide enough for them to haul themselves out of the water. They like to lie on the ice by a hole and bask in the sun while they are moulting. When a hunter finds a seal-hole, he checks to see if it is in use by looking for traces of fur round the hole. Then he will try to find other holes nearby, which other hunters then wait at. They often throw snow into the hole so that the seal won't see them before it surfaces. Everyone remains quiet and motionless with their harpoon at the ready in the hope that a seal will surface at one of the holes.

We ate seal meat most days, and I noticed how Niaqutsiaq's children would smother it with tomato ketchup whenever they could. Joshua, a young Inuk from Arctic Bay, obviously was not too keen on it either. 'You can live on this land food OK,' he told me, 'but it tastes like shit!'

On 25 June, Niaqutsiaq announced that he was going to Igloolik for supplies. We left in the early afternoon and hunted for seals along the way. We arrived in the early evening to find the community almost deserted. School had already ended for the summer and most of the population had moved out to camps. While Niaqutsiaq went to the store to buy supplies, I had time to visit friends and have a welcome shower.

By 10 pm Niaqutsiaq was ready to leave again. With him were his elderly parents, Irngauti and Rebecca, who were coming out to join us at Ikpiugalik. After a winter confined to Igloolik, it must have made a pleasant change for them to spend a few weeks out on the land. In his day, Irngauti had been a good hunter and was famous among the Iglulingmiut for his skill at skinning and butchering caribou.

Throughout June, the camp at Ikpiugalik grew, as more and more families arrived. Levi's parents, Simiuni and Deporah Quanaq, put up their tent next to Niaqutsiaq's, and there was a lot of socializing between the two families. By the end of the month, there were nine tents and upwards of 40 Inuit at Ikpiugalik, most of them related to Niaqutsiaq.

By now, summer had clearly arrived. The thaw had set in and there were streams of meltwater everywhere. Birds were busy nesting and there were northern divers and long-tailed ducks on many of the island's ponds. On one of my walks inland, I counted 64 snow geese grazing by a lake a few miles from our camp.

Most of the time the weather was dreadful. It seemed that almost every day we had fog or rain. This didn't deter Niaqutsiaq from hunting, and most days he returned with at least one seal. Even his mother, who was in her 70s, caught a seal. The children went hunting too, and roamed the tundra searching for birds eggs.

Late one night Andrew and two of Niaqutsiaq's daughters came to my tent, keen to show me what they had found on a ridge behind our camp. There among the rocks was an old grave, and the remains of a wooden coffin was clearly visible. One of the girls prodded at it with a stick and part of the wood fell away, revealing a skull and several bones. The children shrieked and ran away giggling. When I returned to the camp, nobody there knew whose grave it was.

This harsh environment has brought an untimely end to many Inuit lives. In former times the Iglulingmiut buried their dead by wrapping the corpse in a shroud of caribou skin and covering it with snow some distance from the community. In many cases the corpse was then torn to pieces and eaten by wolves, dogs and foxes. If someone died in the summer their body would be covered with rocks. Care was taken to prevent the rocks touching the corpse, and an opening was also left, through which the spirit could escape.

At that time, the Iglulingmiut still retained their own religious beliefs, which held that everything in their world possessed a soul. They believed that when an animal was killed its soul would take over a new body, so it was important not to offend it. There were numerous rituals to ensure this, and they had to be strictly adhered to. For example, when a hunter killed a seal and returned to his igloo, a lump of snow had to be dipped in water and then allowed to drip into the seal's mouth. This was seen as offering a drink to the seal's soul. Like other Inuit groups, the Iglulingmiut also had shamans that they called *angakkuq* who acted as intermediaries between the community and the supernatural forces of the spirit world.

Following the arrival of the first missionaries in the early part of the 1900s, the Iglulingmiut gradually converted to Christianity. At Igloolik both the Anglican and Catholic missionaries competed to convert the Inuit. Apart from their differing forms of Christianity they also brought their prejudices with them. Even today, most Catholics in Igloolik live on the north side of the settlement near their church, while the Anglicans live on the south side near theirs, effectively splitting the community in two. Relationships between the two groups were not always good. One Inuit woman, who comes from a devout Anglican family, told me: 'When I was in my teens, if I so as much looked at a Catholic boy, I would get into big trouble at home.'

By early July, the sea-ice around Jens Munk Island was deteriorating rapidly. Several of the families at our camp had packed up and moved back to Igloolik Island. Niaqutsiaq, Mary and their children decided to go to Gifford Fjord on Baffin Island to hunt caribou, and fish for Arctic char. They didn't find any caribou, so they continued down to the bottom of the fiord to Iqalugasuuvik, which appropriately means 'the place where one goes to fish'. The whole family took turns to jig for Arctic char in an open lead, and managed to catch over 60 fish, many of them large, in only a few hours. Later, back at camp, Niaqutsiaq boiled up a large saucepan of fresh char. It tasted delicious.

With the ice condition worsening, on 10 July, Niaqutsiaq decided that we should move to another camp on the east side of Igloolik Island. He kept his boat there, and wanted to prepare it for summer hunting. We broke camp and managed to pack everything onto two large sleds. Once everything was securely lashed down, Niaqutsiaq started his snowmobile and led the way out onto the sea-ice, while Simiuni, Deporah and their family followed behind. There was over a foot of meltwater on the ice in places and it was obviously going to be a wet journey. He had fastened a piece of plywood across the front of his snowmobile, which acted as an efficient splashguard, but the drive-belt sent up a curtain of spray behind.

We came across several large holes in the ice and some of the leads were already very wide. At one point we were brought to a halt when a lead about 14 feet wide barred our way. For a moment I doubted whether we would be able to cross it. Niaqutsiaq took some extra rope and lengthened the tow-rope that ran between the snowmobile and the sled. We pushed the sled close to the lead until the front of it was at the edge of the ice. Then Niaqutsiaq drove his snowmobile away from the lead, turned and accelerated with full throttle towards it. The snowmobile sent out a curtain of spray as it hit the water and aquaplaned across the surface. I thought it would sink, but the skis hit the ice on the far side and the machine rode up onto it and continued at speed. Seconds later, the tow-rope went taut, the sled jerked, and we hurtled across the lead safely.

It was 3 am by the time we reached Igloolik Point, a popular summer walrus-hunting camp. We put up the tents on the gravel beach close to Niaqutsiaq's upturned boat. By then we were all tired and I just wanted to crawl into my sleeping-bag. In good ice conditions, the journey we had just completed would normally have taken about three hours, but that day it had taken us eight.

By now walrus-hunting seemed to be on most people's minds. The walrus at this time of year are often found at the edge of the pack-ice far out in Foxe Basin. Before the hunters venture out for them, the conditions have to be right. The weather must be good, enough sea-ice must have broken to allow the hunters to reach the walrus, and the temperature has to be warm enough for the meat to ferment afterwards. The main reason that the Iglulingmiut hunt walrus at this time of year is so that they can make the local delicacy *igunaq* (fermented walrus meat).

LEFT Deporah Qaunaq preparing Arctic char for drying at her summer camp at Igloolik Point.

OPPOSITE Aipilik holding a kakivak *(leister) and a lake trout on an autumn fishing-trip.*

For the next week the weather remained bad, with day after day of strong winds, rain and fog. This was fairly typical weather for an Arctic summer, but hopeless for walrus-hunting. During this time, Niaqutsiaq worked on his boat. He also built a rack from driftwood to dry the Arctic char. It took half a day to clean and split all the fish, before they could be hung up and wind-dried. The children played together, spending much of the time exploring the tundra behind the camp and catching lemmings, which they then kept as pets.

On 18 July, Niaqutsiaq woke me at 2 pm to tell me he was going walrus-hunting. I climbed out of my sleeping-bag and stuck my head out of the tent. The weather looked better. It was calm, but there was still some fog. Several of the other hunters were lifting one of the boats onto a sled, as they prepared to take it to the ice edge, about 500 yards away. Niaqutsiaq's boat was already out there. I quickly got dressed and pulled on my rubber boots; then I grabbed my cameras, waterproof trousers and a Parka and went to Niaqutsiaq's tent. I barely had time for a quick mug of coffee and a slice of bannock before we were on our way.

Niaqutsiaq concentrates on steering his boat while out hunting in the summer.

At the ice edge we loaded the boat with gasoline, rifles, harpoons, a Coleman stove and other hunting equipment. I climbed in, together with Limiki, Qammaniq and Attagutalukutuk, who were joining us. Despite spending the entire winter on the beach at Igloolik Point, where it had been exposed to the full force of the elements, the engine spluttered into life after only a few pulls of the starter-cord.

Niaqutsiaq steered the boat slowly away from the ice edge, weaving between the floes. Hunters in two other boats followed in our wake. As soon as we were clear of the ice, Niaqutsiaq opened up the throttle, and we headed out into Foxe Basin. Once we were away from the land, the fog cleared, and despite the strong winds of the previous few days the water was surprisingly calm. This was largely due to the amount of sea-ice that was still around.

After three hours we saw the pack-ice ahead of us, and as we got close Niaqutsiaq cut his speed. We separated from the other boats and slowly made our way along the edge of the pack-ice, winding our way between the floes. We soon spotted a small group of walruses on a floe. The hunters ignored this first group, because the animals were too small. We moved on in search of larger walrus. Later we came across another

ABOVE RIGHT *Walrus in the pack-ice of Foxe Basin.*

BELOW RIGHT *An Inuk aims his rifle at a seal from a freighter canoe during a summer hunt.*

group. This time Niaqutsiaq steered the boat towards them, approaching cautiously. He wanted to get as close as possible, to ensure that the walrus were killed outright while they were still on the ice, because if a seriously wounded walrus got into the water it would probably die and sink before the hunters could reach it.

As we approached, several of the animals slithered into the water and surfaced close to our boat. I was apprehensive, as I had heard tales of walrus attacking boats. Seconds later, the hunters opened fire, killing two animals outright. I was surprised to see that several of the walrus in the water had not swum away after the shooting.

As I bent down to get another lens from my camera-bag, I noticed that we were taking in a lot of water. In the excitement, we had not realized that we had been attacked by a walrus. Niaqutsiaq drove the boat to a nearby floe and we hauled it up onto the ice. A quick inspection of the hull revealed a substantial hole made by a walrus' tusk. With customary ingenuity, Niaqutsiaq cut a suitably sized patch from a plastic bottle and nailed it over the hole.

Niaqutsiaq butchers a walrus on an ice-floe in Foxe Basin.

Later, we shot two more walrus, and then the hard work began. First, we had to tow the dead animals to a flat piece of ice, haul them up, butcher them, and prepare the meat for making *igunaq*. Bags were made from large pieces of walrus skin, and these were stuffed with meat and fat before being laced up with thin lengths of walrus hide. By the time the bags were closed, they looked like large cylindrical sausages, about 28 inches long and 12 in diameter.

It took about five hours to finish butchering the meat. Then we boiled up some of the liver, heart and intestines to eat while we waited for the other hunters to return. It was not long before we saw them approaching. They had also shot some walrus, a little further north.

We brewed tea and then began loading the meat. By midnight we were on our way, the boats were loaded to the gunwales, as we headed back towards Igloolik Island. It was a beautiful sunny night; the sea was like glass and there were seabirds feeding everywhere.

By 4 am we were once again negotiating the ice-floes around Igloolik Island, and not long afterwards we reached the ice edge off Igloolik Point. Several young men drove snowmobiles out to the boats and helped us unload the meat. It was divided up, put onto the sleds, and driven back to camp. Later, pits were dug in the gravel and the bags of meat placed in them and covered over. There they would be left to ferment for several months. In October, or perhaps later, the first bags of *igunaq* would be dug up again and eaten. It would probably last Niaqutsiaq and his family for most of the winter. In Igloolik, *igunaq*, like all land food, is shared among the relatives of the hunters.

By mid-August the walrus season would be over. Niaqutsiaq and his family would move to Gifford Fjord to fish for Arctic char and hunt caribou. The Iglulingmiut consider the late summer to be the best time to hunt caribou, as by then they usually have back-fat on them and their fur is right for making winter clothes.

One evening, Mary told me that she and Niaqutsiaq had decided to give up their outpost-camp life on Baffin Island. They planned to move back to Igloolik at the end of the summer. Niaqutsiaq would continue to hunt out of Igloolik, as well as taking carpentry work whenever he could find it in town. Later, Mary managed to get a job working in the Co-op store, and their children attended school.

One of the most important aspects of the Community Harvester Assistance Programme is that it gives the Inuit a choice. They don't have to be part of the wage-earning community, and it enables them to get away from the social problems that exist in many of the settlements. Outpost camps also often have the advantage of being in better locations for hunting and gathering food. Above all the Community Harvester Assistance Programme is helping to preserve the Inuit culture. Children are able to travel with their parents and learn the skills necessary to survive in the harsh Arctic environment. Outpost-camp life helps to cement the strong bond that exists between the Inuit and the land, and helps them to retain their cultural identity. While I was with the Taqqaugaqs at their outpost camp at Iglurjuat, their son Luke told me: 'When I am here, I feel like an Inuk; at Igloolik, I don't.'

The Nenets of Siberia
Reindeer-herders at the End of the Earth

The Yamal Peninsula is about the size of Britain – a vast, flat and largely featureless area of tundra that protrudes 450 miles from the north coast of Siberia into the Arctic Ocean. In winter, temperatures sink as low as -58°F (-50°C), and the peninsula is lashed by strong winds for much of the year. From the air it looks like an unforgiving wilderness, yet the Yamal has been home to the Nenets and their reindeer herds for over 1,000 years. It was, in fact, they who named this bleak and isolated area of the Russian North Yamal, which appropriately means 'the end of the earth'.

The exact ancestry of the Nenets is still unclear, although their language belongs to the Samoyedic linguistic group, linking them to peoples as far south as Turkey. Reindeer-breeding is thought to have been introduced into the Yamal during the tenth century by the ancestors of today's Nenets. It is a form of pastoralism that has changed relatively little in the past 1,000 years. The herders and their deer spend the winter in the forests south of the River Ob. Here the reindeer feed on moss and lichen, to which they dig down, clearing away the snow with their hooves. Each March they begin the migration to their summer pastures in the north of the peninsula, a 600-mile journey that takes them three months to complete. There, the reindeer fatten on lush grasses

ABOVE A shy girl in front of her family's summer tent.

LEFT A Nenet woman, dressed up against the cold, rests against a sled during a day's travel.

Tanya, accompanied by her daughter, drives a reindeer sled during the migration.

and the cold winds off the Kara Sea keep the summer temperatures low and limit the number of mosquitoes. In late August, they begin the long return journey to their winter pastures.

These arduous bi-annual treks benefit both the reindeer and the herders. At their winter pastures, reindeer live almost exclusively on lichen, which is mainly carbohydrate. Although lichen can sustain reindeer, and they can even grow fat on it, they need protein for growth; this they get from the green pastures in the north of the Yamal Peninsula. The migration enables the herders to conserve their fragile and slow-growing lichen pastures for winter. It is estimated that grazed lichen takes 10–20 years to recover, as the growth-rate is only about 1/2 inch per year.

In the Yamal today, there are some 2,460 Nenet herding families who together manage a total of about 476,000 reindeer. These Nenet reindeer-herders have probably the most intact native culture to be found anywhere in the Arctic today. Although they were persecuted under Stalin and the Communists, who changed their herds from private to state-owned, their life out on the tundra changed very little. In some ways, isolation from the outside world under the Communist regime of the former Soviet Union may have helped to preserve the Nenet culture. As a consequence, no missionaries were allowed into the Yamal, and today many Nenet herders still believe in their own god and animistic religion.

With the fall of Communism, a combination of Russian and foreign interests have begun seriously to exploit the vast gasfields of the Yamal. The tundra is extremely fragile and already large areas of the Nenets' traditional lands have been polluted and damaged by heavy machinery. This has seriously affected the life of the reindeer-herders, who now on their migrations have to cross pipelines, roads, and tundra strewn with debris. Whether the Nenet reindeer-herding culture will be able to withstand this type of twentieth-century intrusion into their nomadic lifestyle remains to be seen.

. . . .

I stood guard over our bags outside the terminal building at Salekhard airport while my assistant Nik disappeared inside to join the crush of bodies that surrounded the ticket counter. Salekhard, a town of 30,000 people, lies at the mouth of the River Ob in western Siberia. We had arrived from Moscow a couple of days earlier, and now planned to fly to the small community of Panayevsk on the Yamal Peninsula.

The airport was shabby, and on the approach road there were several old aircraft mounted on concrete plinths, presumably as a tribute to Soviet aviation. Among these was an Antonov-2, an old biplane from the 1940s with canvas-covered wings. It was widely used throughout the Siberian North.

A herder driving a reindeer sled during a race at a spring festival.

A woman and child emerge from their reindeer-skin tent after a winter storm.

Nik disappeared into a throng of Russians, wrapped in bulky furs, to try to find our contact. Half an hour later he returned, looking dismayed and without tickets. He told me, with a shrug of resignation, that there was no sign of our contact and maybe we would not fly today. It was frustrating as the weather was perfect, -22°F (-30°C) with clear skies and not a breath of wind. We deliberated what to do for a while. To me it was clear – we should go back to our hotel and try again tomorrow. Nik, however, had other ideas and disappeared back inside the terminal building.

Within an hour we were on a plane taxiing down the runway. It was only then that Nik explained that a 'gift' of a few dollars and some American cigarettes had secured us space on an already full plane. He also revealed, to my dismay, that the plane was not going to Panayevsk, as I had thought, but to a community further north called Yar-Sale.

As the engines began to roar, it suddenly dawned on me that the plane we were on was an Antonov-2, the same type that I had seen mounted on a plinth at the airport. I fumbled around for a seat-belt, but abandoned the idea after only finding one half. 'What the hell,' I thought, 'nobody else is wearing them anyway.' I resigned myself to the fact that I was about to take off in a biplane that was old enough to have been in a museum, that was overloaded, and that was flying to the wrong destination anyway.

Despite my apprehension, we landed safely at Yar-Sale an hour later, where we met up with Dmitrij Khorolya. Dmitrij is a native Siberian, a Nenet, who at the age of 32 had become director of the Yarsalinskij State Farm – the largest in Russia. Our timing was fortunate. In a few days, Dmitrij told me, a helicopter would be flying to some of the herding camps and he could arrange for us to be dropped off at one of them.

Two days later, on a blustery cold day, we climbed aboard an MI-8 helicopter along with 15 other passengers who were mainly reindeer-herders returning to their camps. There was a strong smell of stale vodka and I just hoped it was not coming from the cockpit. Despite being a large helicopter, there was little free space because the fuselage was crammed with supplies for the herding camps. Several of the passengers ended up sitting on sacks of frozen fish and bread.

We flew south over snow-covered tundra, punctuated with ponds frozen solid by the winter's cold. After an hour, trees began to appear in an otherwise bleak landscape. Slowly we made the transition from windswept open tundra to the spruce forests of the *taiga*, and then we began to descend. As we circled a clearing I rubbed the frost from the window and peered out once more. The view was breathtaking. At the edge of a spruce forest, hundreds of reindeer grazed around a herders' camp, while children dressed from head to foot in furs played in the snow outside teepee-style tents. It looked like a winter scene from some bygone age, and I found it difficult to believe that this was western Siberia in the 1990s.

As the swirling cloud of snow, thrown up by the rotors of the departing helicopter, settled, I got my first good look at the camp. There were six tents erected in a line and around them there was a clutter of sleds and equipment. The official title of this reindeer-herding group was Brigade No. 8, and it comprised nine families who worked

Reindeer mill around a herders' camp in the forest near Kutop'yugan.

together to manage some 4,500 reindeer. I was met by Sergei Serotetto, the group's leader, who invited us back to his tent. Inside it was dim but surprisingly snug, with heat provided by a small wood-stove. The tent wall was a double layer of reindeer hide, which offered excellent insulation against Siberia's winter cold.

We sat cross-legged on reindeer skins as Sergei's wife, Galya, served us a meal of raw reindeer meat, bread and hot tea. The spacious tent was home to two families. As we sat eating, there was a steady stream of adults and children entering and leaving. Sergei lived on one side with his wife and children, while the other side was occupied by his brother Sasha and his family. Their mother, Yakhaney, also lived with them. After the meal, we stretched out on the reindeer skins. Sergei told me that the place we were camped at was called Oyata-To ('island in the lake'). They had been in the area for a month, and in a day or two they would begin their migration northwards to their summer pastures, an arduous 600-mile journey by reindeer sled which would involve the crossing of 11 major rivers and take them three months to complete.

I was ill-prepared for this type of winter travel. On my journey to the Yamal, one of my bags containing my sleeping-bag and most of my cold-weather clothing had gone astray. Once they learned of my predicament, Galya and Sasha's wife Tanya lost little time in finding me substitute clothing. They visited several of the other families and came back with an assortment of reindeer-skin clothing for me to try on. I was soon kitted out with a pair of *pimy* (thigh-length reindeer-skin boots) and a *malitsa* (a long-hooded Parka worn with the fur facing inwards). These clothes were very comfortable and would keep me warm even in the worst Siberian winter weather.

In the afternoon, as the watery golden sun set behind the spruce trees, the camp was a hive of activity. Several of the men were busy building new sleds and repairing old ones for the migration. The Nenets' sleds are beautiful and ideally suited to the conditions. They are hand-crafted using the simplest of homemade tools, such as bow-drills, knives and chisels. The men worked until dark. There was a sense of urgency in finishing the sleds, as once we were north of the tree-line there would be no more wood.

Meanwhile, the women were carrying out their seemingly unending chores of chopping firewood, collecting snow to melt for water and scraping birch logs to make shavings. These are used for toilet paper and nappies.

In the evening, the tent was filled with the smell of cooking reindeer meat as Galya and Tanya prepared a meal. Although they shared a tent, both families ate separately. Afterwards, we sat and talked for a while, and then Sasha went to take his turn at keeping watch over the herd, something that all the men do in shifts. It is important to keep the reindeer together and protect them from predators. It's tough work, and even in the middle of winter the men don't use any shelter. When they need to rest they just lie out in the open on their sled. I didn't envy Sasha that night, as it was bitterly cold with a biting north wind. As we got ready to turn in, Galya arranged the skins for us to sleep on. As I had no sleeping-bag, Galya, Tanya and Yakhaney lent me their *yagushkas* (reindeer-

A woman scraping a log. The shavings will be used for babies' nappies and toilet paper.

162

skin coats) to cover myself with. These coats, with their double layer of reindeer skin, kept me warm throughout the night.

Yakhaney was up first. She stoked the fire and put a kettle of water on to heat. Gradually everyone in the tent woke up. We drank hot tea and ate raw fish and bread for breakfast, while Sergei and Sasha's daughters, Neseinye and Christina, slept on. Apart from Sergei's teenage son Leova, they were the only children in our tent; the others were at boarding-school in Yar-Sale.

Outside there was the sound of chopping wood as the other families began their day. It was a cold, clear morning and the tents were covered in hoar-frost. Sergei left camp early to check on the main herd. The reindeer that milled around our camp were draft animals that were used to being handled and were used for pulling sleds. Some were so tame they would wander nonchalantly around the camp on the lookout for food. They were great opportunists. On one occasion I was in Sergei's tent when I heard a commotion outside. I emerged in time to see a reindeer running away with a Nenet woman in hot pursuit. Its head was held high and a sack of bread was firmly clenched between its teeth. The Nenets seemed to care for their reindeer, and even in moments of intense frustration I never saw them lose their temper. Some of the reindeer round our camp were sick yearlings, often fed and cared for by the children.

OPPOSITE *Inside a reindeer-skin tent, a woman makes tea on a wood-burning stove.*

BELOW *A Nenet woman feeds two sick yearling reindeer.*

To begin with, I wondered why whenever I left Sergei's tent reindeer would quickly gather round me, even after dark. The reason, I soon discovered, was their craving for human urine, which provides them with salts they cannot otherwise obtain in the winter. Some scientists believe that this may have played a role in the domestication of reindeer.

During the morning, Neseinye played outside with her cousin Christina, while the rest of the family worked around the camp preparing for the migration. Many of the children's games, I discovered, were based on reindeer-herding. They practised lassoing and hunting with bow and arrow. In another game, the children split into two groups, one pretending to be reindeer and the other herders.

LEFT Herders killing a reindeer for food. An average family eats 80 reindeer a year.

OPPOSITE After killing a reindeer for food, herders drink the blood of the animal.

Around midday, one of the herders returned to camp, leading a bull reindeer, which was then killed and butchered. Everyone gathered round the carcass, cutting off slices of meat and drinking the blood from a white china cup. I joined in, gulping down a cup of the blood as quickly as I could. This was not a drink I felt inclined to sip and savour. A week before I had met a Russian doctor who had encouraged me to drink reindeer blood while I was out on the tundra, saying: 'It is very healthy, and rich in vitamins and minerals.'

On 14 March our camp came to life at first light. Today we would begin the migration north to the summer pastures. There was no apparent excitement at the start of such a long journey; for the Nenet herders it was almost routine. Sergei had been making this annual 600-mile trip for the past 23 years. While the women broke camp and began to load the sleds, the men rounded up the 900 draft reindeer and drove

them into a makeshift corral made of sleds and netting. Then members of each family went into the corral to catch reindeer to pull their sleds. Most of the reindeer just stood quietly; they seemed relatively tame, and were obviously used to being handled. It took over four hours to catch and harness the 300 reindeer that were needed to pull all the sleds. Many of the harnesses had fittings made from mammoth ivory. The Nenets find the ivory during the summer months out on the tundra, and use it for making everything from buttons to knife handles and tobacco boxes.

By midday all the sleds were packed and the reindeer hitched up and ready to move. We ate some raw fish and bread, and drank hot tea, before setting off. Sergei warned me that we had a long journey ahead of us. A forest fire had destroyed a large area of lichen north of us, and it was 30 miles to the next pastures where the reindeer could feed.

The migration began without ceremony. Sergei simply led the way, driving his reindeer across the clearing, up a slope and into the spruce forest. One by one the other members of the group followed. Most of the equipment and supplies were carried on trains of sleds, driven mainly by the women and older men. The younger men drove single sleds and kept the reindeer from straying. The reindeer moved at a steady pace, following Sergei's trail as it wound through the forest. I soon discovered that a reindeer

A herder selects a draft reindeer which he will use to pull one of his sleds.

Nenaneya sewing a pair of reindeer-skin boots in her family's tent.

sled was a wonderful way to travel through this fairy-tale winter landscape. The soft jingling of the bells on the harnesses of the reindeer, the clicking of their tendons and the swish of the sled-runners against the snow were the only sounds. High above us at the top of one of the spruce trees a solitary capercaillie sat eyeing us, unperturbed, as we slowly passed by. We must have been an impressive sight, a meandering line of 120 reindeer sleds stretching back for over a mile.

It took us eight hours to cover the 30 miles to our next campsite near the Yarudey River, and it was almost dark by the time we arrived. In the dim twilight the tents were quickly erected.

Each of the family tents was large, consisting of 39 long spruce poles and a double-layered covering, made from 60 separate reindeer skins. The tents are so well made that they can last for over 50 years. Because of the large number of skins used, they are extremely valuable to the Nenets. It takes about five sleds to transport each family's tent and possessions.

The organization of making camp is fascinating. Once the campsite has been selected, the women take charge of the whole procedure, erecting the tent and laying out the family's possessions inside. The women are meticulous and, after each day's travelling, I found that my rucksack was always placed in exactly the same position.

Within an hour of arriving at the new campsite, our tent was up and a pot of reindeer-meat stew was already simmering on the stove. Over a very welcome hot meal, Sergei explained that we would rest the next day, and then, weather permitting, we would move on.

The next morning Yakhaney was up, as usual, at first light, putting wood on the stove while everyone else slept on after the exertions of the previous day. Sergei seemed much more relaxed and played with Neseinye. The cloud and snow had cleared to reveal a sunny and cold morning, with hoar-frost sparkling on the spruce trees. The snow around our camp was deep where it had not been trampled by the reindeer and we used heavy wooden skis to move around. For the men who were not watching over the herd, it was a day to relax. The women seemed to be working as hard as ever just to keep ahead of their camp chores.

That morning, Leova returned to camp disgruntled. He had been asleep on his sled, after keeping watch over the herd, and had tied his dog to his ankle so that he would be woken immediately if a wolf came near. Much to the amusement of everyone else, Tanya had unwittingly called the dog in order to feed it, which resulted in Leova being rudely awakened as the dog struggled to return to camp for its food.

The life of Nenet herders is governed by a whole range of taboos. To begin with, I was baffled by the fact that, whenever I took my reindeer-skin boots off in the tent, they would disappear from where I had left them. Later I learnt that there was a specific area within the tent for men's boots to be kept and another for women's. The women seem to be affected by more taboos than men. For example, women are not permitted to walk over a lasso or a reindeer harness. Another taboo involves an invisible line that stretches from the centre of each tent to the back, and then theoretically on into infinity. Women are prohibited from crossing this line.

In the afternoon we had some visitors. They were herders from another brigade, who were camped some two hours' travelling away from us. Much of their migration route ran parallel with ours, and so members of both groups regularly visited each other. All visitors were offered the traditional hospitality of hot tea as well as a meal of raw reindeer meat or fish. It was an opportunity for the herders to socialize and exchange news and gossip.

The next day we awoke to an unseasonably warm southerly wind, and rain beat down on our tent. Rain at this time of the year was worrying to the herders, who feared that it could lead to the lichen pastures icing over. Reindeer are adept at scraping deep snow off the tundra with their hooves to reach the lichen below, but ice could make this impossible. Fortunately, it was only a brief shower and the skies soon cleared.

On the morning of 19 March, we broke camp and prepared to move. Once again the sleds were packed, the draft reindeer gathered and harnessed, and we set off at midday heading north. We passed the remains of one of Stalin's many labour-camps; some posts and wire sticking up through the snow were all that remained. It was hard to imagine a more desolate and inhospitable place to be incarcerated. A short while later, we crossed the railway line that Stalin had ordered to be built to link the town of Vorkuta on the west side of the Ural mountains with the Yenisey River in the east. The working conditions were so severe that over 100,000 forced labourers died during the construction of this railway, which was never completed.

With the railway behind us, we crossed the frozen Yarudey River and then began to climb again up onto higher ground. As we continued our journey through this Siberian wilderness, we passed a Nenet shrine. All that was visible was a pile of snow-covered reindeer antlers almost 6 feet high. The Nenets' religion has survived both Stalin's purges and 70 years of Communism. The herders still practise an animistic religion and worship their own god, Num. Their religious practices are kept very low-key. Each group has idols that are stored on a sled, kept close to the leader's tent. The sled with the idols is pulled by sacred reindeer, always immediately behind the leader's sled. Most families also keep an idol in their tent. This is called *yaminga* ('mother of the land'), which protects them and wards off evil spirits. On a visit to the 4th Brigade's camp on one occasion, I visited Nudyarney, an 85-year-old woman. When I raised the subject of idols, she produced her *yaminga*. It was a wooden doll that she kept wrapped up in an old piece of crimson cloth. The doll was dressed in three miniature *yagushkas* and had three belts, one for each of the three children that had been born in the tent.

The next move turned out to be shorter and less arduous. We covered the 15 miles to the next pastures in a little over four hours, and then we made camp once again.

By now a distinctive pattern had developed to the migration: move one day, rest a day or maybe two, and then move on again. The scenery was magnificent. Our route took us through forests where the snow was waist-deep, and across frozen lakes and tundra where winds had etched patterns into the surface of the hard-packed snow. As we gradually headed north, the trees became smaller and more spread out.

OVERLEAF Women travelling by reindeer sled across the tundra during a winter storm.

BELOW A woman drives a train of reindeer sleds during the spring migration.

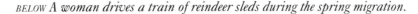

By the end of March, the rhythm of our travel was broken when we camped in the forest near Kutop'yugan, only a few miles south of the frozen River Ob. The Ob represents a formidable obstacle for the herders and their reindeer. At its mouth, where we would cross, it was 37 miles wide. It was a long way beyond that to the next lichen pastures where the reindeer could feed, so it was important that the reindeer were well rested and the weather was good before we made the crossing. The Ob marks the northern limit of the tree-line. Once across the river, there would be no more forests, just hundreds of miles of open tundra all the way to the summer pastures in the north of the Yamal Peninsula.

We spent three days near Kutop'yugan while the reindeer rested and we waited for good weather. It turned into quite a social time for the herders, with a steady stream of visitors coming to our camp from the nearby village. They brought us some badly needed bread, which was greatly appreciated, as we were surviving almost exclusively on a diet of reindeer meat and fish. One of our visitors was an 85-year-old man called Porngui Numsi ('old man'). His father had been a shaman who, like many other shamans, was imprisoned and died in one of Stalin's camps. Porngui kept everyone amused for hours, as he related stories from the days of his youth.

One morning I trudged up a slope to photograph our camp at dawn. The sun had only just risen over the horizon, spilling golden light onto the snow-covered scene. In the still air, smoke gently curled from the tops of the tents as the herders began their day. The scene had a magical quality. Even though I had been with these herders for almost a month now, I continued to be amazed by just how traditional they were. After more than 20 years of photographing Arctic peoples, I was not expecting to find a culture this intact, particularly in the former Soviet Union.

Later that afternoon, Sasha loaded three reindeer carcasses onto his sled and drove to Kutop'yugan to try to sell the meat to a local shopkeeper. A few hours later, he returned with the carcasses still on his sled. 'They only offered me one hundred roubles [about 14 American cents at the time], a kilo [2.2 pounds], but they sell it for three hundred,' Sasha complained, before adding, 'that's the Russian Mafia!' It was not difficult to see why both Sergei and Sasha looked back on the Communist era as the good old days. 'Under Brezhnev things were good for us,' Sasha told me. 'We had everything we needed; now we can't even afford to buy a bottle of vodka.'

Many of the reindeer herds in the Yamal were being privatized and were no longer owned by the state farms. In our herd, some 3,000 reindeer were still owned by the state farm; the remaining 1,500 were owned by the herders themselves. Nenet herders like Sergei and Sasha have experienced no benefit from the move towards privatization, largely because no real market has been developed for their reindeer meat. Despite this, it seemed to me that, in these difficult economic times, many Nenet herders had a better life than most Russians, particularly those living in the big cities. Although reindeer-herding is a tough way of life, the Nenets have as much meat and fish as they need, and out on the tundra they are more or less free to conduct their lives as they wish.

On 28 March, the weather was finally good enough to cross the River Ob. We got up at 1.30 am to begin our day's travel, breaking camp and packing sleds in the dark. It was cold and clear and an array of Northern Lights shimmered in the night sky. At the first light of dawn, the draft reindeer were rounded up and the slow process of catching and harnessing them began. By sunrise we were on our way through the forest. After only a few miles the trees finally ended, and there in front of us was the vast and frozen River Ob, its far bank still out of sight.

No longer constrained by narrow, winding forest trails, we were able to harness extra reindeer to the sleds. Most of the group now used four instead of three reindeer to pull their sleds. Sasha had five. 'Today I have a Mercedes!' he yelled exuberantly, as he sped past me. After a while the main herd followed us down onto the frozen river. It was only then that I got my first view of the entire herd. It was a spectacular sight, a mass of 4,500 reindeer following our meandering trail across the ice.

A reindeer-herders' camp at sunrise near Kutop'yugan.

Sergei with his daughter during a tea-break on the spring migration.

At noon we stopped for a welcome rest and a chance to warm up with a quick meal of bread, reindeer meat and hot tea. Sergei pointed to a bank of freezing fog that was rolling in. Within an hour the visibility was dramatically reduced and it became bitterly cold. Everywhere was white, and with no visible horizon it was as if we were travelling across a blank sheet of paper. For ten hours the reindeer trudged slowly onwards across the frozen river. I only realized that we had reached the north side of the Ob when we passed some brush willow sticking up through the snow; but we still had some way to go to the nearest pastures where the reindeer could feed. We changed direction and headed east along the course of a small river, before beginning a gradual climb up onto the rolling tundra. It was evening by the time we reached our new campsite, and the fog that enshrouded us was turned from white to gold by the setting sun. It had taken us 14 hours to travel 47 miles, and there was an atmosphere of exhausted relief as we once again made camp.

After the long and tiring crossing of the River Ob, the reindeer needed several days to rest and feed. This gave the herders the opportunity to visit the village of Yar-Sale, which was only 15 miles away. The herders in our group spend virtually the entire year out on the tundra with the reindeer. Most of them, however, have homes as well

ABOVE RIGHT *A herd of 4,000 reindeer crossing the frozen River Ob during the spring migration.*

BELOW RIGHT *A woman leads a train of reindeer sleds down an icy slope near the River Ob.*

as family and friends in Yar-Sale, which they look on as their village. The herders usually only have the opportunity to visit Yar-Sale twice a year – once on their way north in the spring, and then again on their way back south in the autumn. For them, a visit to Yar-Sale was an exciting break. It offered them the chance to meet up with friends and relations and also to pick up essential supplies of tea, bread, tobacco, and so on, that they could buy with credit from the state farm. It also gave them the opportunity of seeing their older children, who attended the boarding-school there, and who would join them after school finished at the end of May.

The next morning there was an atmosphere of excitement as several of us got ready to go to town. The women looked elegant in their best *yagushkas* as we left in a convoy of reindeer sleds for Yar-Sale. The Nenet women decorate their fine furs with exquisite patterns, made by inlaying small pieces of different-coloured reindeer skin.

For me, Yar-Sale was the end of the journey, but Sergei and the other herders still had another 370 miles ahead of them before reaching their reindeers' summer pastures. Now they had to push on quickly before the snow melted from the land. By

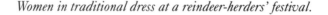

Women in traditional dress at a reindeer-herders' festival.

the end of April, the females would begin calving, and Sergei wanted to be able to cross as many rivers as possible while they were still frozen, to avoid the young calves having to swim. Reindeer-herding, I discovered, has its own set of pressures and problems.

The source of one of the main problems being faced by herders in the Yamal lies some 4,500 feet beneath their reindeers' feet. Locked under all the Yamal's snow and ice lie vast deposits of natural gas, an estimated 45 trillion cubic feet! The gas was first discovered in the 1960s, and since that time Russia's state gas company, Gasprom, has been responsible for surveying and sinking hundreds of test wells in the Yamal. Environmentalists blame Gasprom for the appalling environmental damage. An estimated 2,500 square miles of tundra has been ruined in the past ten years alone. Gashes have been carved all over the tundra's fragile surface by trucks and heavy machines. Lakes have been polluted by oil and toxic chemicals used for lubricating the drills. Seventy per cent of the machinery used in the gasfields has broken down and been discarded, turning large areas of the tundra into one vast scrapyard of rusting metal. In spite of all the exploration and drilling, the Yamal has yet to produce any natural gas. The reason for this is that, in the past, Russia lacked both the technology and the hard cash that was necessary. They also had no real market for gas.

The recent political changes in the former Soviet Union have paved the way for western oil and gas companies to move in to 'help' Russia develop its energy resources. The American corporation Amoco is one of the front-runners, and it plans to enter into partnership with Russia's Gasprom to develop the gasfields in the Yamal. It's a grand scheme, which involves the building of a 300-mile road and railway, the construction of an offshore terminal, and a 1,500-mile pipeline. This may be good news for Russia's ailing economy, and for the employees and shareholders of a number of western companies, but for the Nenet reindeer-herders it is a potential disaster that threatens to drive them and their reindeer off the tundra for ever.

The first area to be developed for natural-gas production is the field at Bovanenkovo. To date, it's the most significant gas discovery on the Yamal Peninsula. 'We are talking gigantic,' one Amoco employee told me. 'Bovanenkovo has three-quarters as much gas as all the gasfields in the United States combined.'

For Sergei Serotetto and his fellow herders, the gas development at Bovanenkovo is a major concern. His herding group and several others have their summer pastures close to the gasfield. It's unlikely that gas will be produced there before 1998, but it's already causing the herders problems.

During the time I spent with Sergei and Sasha they often spoke of the problems they were experiencing now, and their concerns for the future. They told me of the difficulties of trying to drive reindeer herds across raised roads, over pipelines and through rows of electricity poles; how gas workers poach their reindeer when they want fresh meat; and about the dogs kept at drilling sites which often kill and maim the reindeer; and how helicopter crews, searching for artifacts made of mammoth ivory, raid the herders' depots where they leave their winter sleds and clothes during the summer. It was not difficult to see why herders like Sergei were upset.

Before I left Yar-Sale, Sergei and his family visited me to say goodbye. As we sat drinking tea together, he told me of the meetings he had attended in Yar-Sale with bureaucrats and gas company officials. He was not happy with what he had heard, and he obviously didn't trust the gas companies. 'It's very bad what they are doing at Bovanenkovo,' he told me, shaking his head from side to side. 'You should come back in the summer and see for yourself.'

A few days later, as I left Yar-Sale, I knew that Sergei was right – the only way I could fully understand the threats facing this extraordinary culture was to return in the summer and see Bovanenkovo for myself. I then decided to make every effort to return to the Yamal, so I could join Sergei and his group as they travelled with their reindeer through the gasfields.

· · · · · · ·

In early August, I found myself flying over the Yamal once again. It looked like a very different world to the icy waste I had left in April. The landscape was mottled green and russet with countless small lakes that sparkled in the sunshine. Flying over old drilling sites, I could see they were surrounded by discarded machinery and other debris. Everywhere there were scars on the land where heavy trucks and bulldozers had broken through the fragile surface of the tundra. It would take decades to heal.

It was mid-afternoon when the helicopter began to circle over a Nenet herders' camp. As we began to descend, I could see six tents, and by a lake nearby a herd of draft reindeer were corralled. A few minutes later I was on the ground, being welcomed once more by Sergei and the rest of the group. I was happy to be back among them.

The group had increased to about 50 people, largely as the result of the schoolchildren joining their families during the summer break. The reindeer appeared to have benefitted from their summer grazing. They were fat and sleek and they looked impressive with their antlers in velvet.

The Nenets were now using their summer tents, which were lighter and made from cloth rather than reindeer skin. They had also dispensed with the stoves, and cooking was now done over an open fire in the centre of the tent, with brush willow being used for fuel.

Later, as we sat in Sergei's tent eating reindeer meat, he told me that the calving had gone well in April and they had not had a bad summer. So far, they had managed to avoid having any of their reindeer killed by the gas workers or their dogs. But it was not all good news; they were concerned that they had not been able to catch any fish. In the past, Sergei told me, they had always been able to catch plenty of fish in the Seyakha River, which runs through the gasfield. This year there were none in the river or in nearby lakes. 'The gas workers net the river. Maybe there are no fish left or the river is polluted now,' Sergei said, with a shrug of resignation. 'It's not good,' Sasha added, 'to eat only reindeer meat day after day.' They told me that we were west of

Bovanenkovo and they were just starting the long journey back south to the winter pastures. In a few days, they would have to drive their reindeer back through the gasfields.

We talked late into the night, and when I awoke the next morning both Sergei and Sasha had left to check on the main herd. Galya and Tanya spent the morning busily softening reindeer skins that would later be made into clothes. Even very young children helped their parents with camp chores. Neseinye, who was only six, was busy working at softening a reindeer skin, alongside her mother. When the men corralled the draft reindeer close to the camp, young boys would grab their own lassos and walk fearlessly amongst the reindeer even though they were dwarfed by the large bulls. When they were not helping their parents, they were usually out playing on the tundra or gathering berries.

After two days of rain and cold northerly winds, we broke camp, corralled the reindeer and prepared to move. The herders were using their summer sleds, which were much lighter and more suitable for travelling on snow-free tundra. I hitched a ride on a sled, pulled by five reindeer, that was driven very competently by Sasha's ten-year-old son, Alexei.

A boy practises his lassoing out on the summer tundra.

The landscape was beautiful, with swaying cotton grass in all directions. The tundra was already showing the effects of the first autumn frosts and the grasses had begun to turn golden brown. It was cold, with a northwesterly wind blowing straight off the Kara Sea, but at least there were no mosquitoes. We travelled slowly, stopping frequently along the way to rest the reindeer. At each stop, the children would jump off the sleds and dash across the tundra in search of cloudberries. Once we were on the move again, they would have to run to catch up.

After only a couple of hours, we made camp on high ground overlooking a lake. From our camp Sasha pointed to a tiny distant vertical shape on the horizon. Through binoculars I could see that it was a drilling rig. We were nearing the gasfield.

The next day we moved again, setting off in the afternoon. This time I travelled with Sasha, who led the way, heading east across the tundra. Sasha's dog trotted along beside us, making hunting forays into clumps of brush willow, occasionally causing an explosion of ptarmigan that flew off in all directions.

After three hours of slow travel, we camped again on high ground. By now 11 drilling rigs were clearly visible in the distance; we were under 6 miles from Bovanenkovo. As we made camp, Sasha watched with dismay as the reindeer quickly

Reindeer grazing at their summer pastures in the Yamal Peninsula.

Surrounded by reindeer, a girl stands on a sled at the summer pastures.

scattered in all directions. The problem, he explained, was that reindeer have a passion for wild mushrooms. In years when there is an abundance of mushrooms, the herders have no problem, because the reindeer tend to stay together and graze, but this year mushrooms were scarce, causing the reindeer to scatter in search of the fungi. For the herders this meant extra work trying to keep the herd together.

Just before sunset, I joined Sasha as he went to set a fishing net on a lake close to our camp. It was a beautiful spot. The grass was waist-high at the water's edge, and two northern divers flew off as we approached. Sasha assured me that this lake was full of big fish.

The following morning I went back to the lake with Sasha to check the net. He was surprised and dismayed to find it empty. 'In the past we always caught fish here every year,' he told me. 'Now they have disappeared.' Sasha suspected that gas-company workers were responsible, complaining, 'they throw dynamite into the lakes to catch fish.'

Later that day, Sasha decided to go to one of the drilling rigs to try to sell some reindeer meat. He had no success, and arrived back at sunset. The gas workers, it seemed, were worse off than the Nenets. Some had not been paid for four months and had no money. They had even run out of bread and potatoes and had nothing to barter with.

For the next two days we skirted the edge of the gasfield. Sergei was the most tense that I had seen him and he was clearly anxious about the herd. He had good reason to be worried. We had to negotiate a pipeline and two raised roads, which were difficult to get the reindeer and sleds across. The herders needed to be constantly

Draft reindeer swim across the Seyakha River as they head south on the autumn migration.

vigilant to protect the reindeer from the workers' dogs, which ran wild. Each day there was some incident or another: a reindeer cut a hoof on a piece of sharp metal left lying on the tundra; one animal got caught up in some discarded coils of wire. There was rusting debris everywhere.

The evening of 18 August found us camped on a high ridge overlooking another major obstacle – a natural one this time. Sergei and the other herders had encountered the Seyakha River many times before, and, providing the weather was good enough, the herd would swim across the next day. From our campsite we could see 14 drilling rigs. 'You see,' Sergei said, pointing out across the gasfield, 'How they put their drilling rigs on all the best high ground that is dry, so we have to put our tents in the low places where it is wet.'

The next morning I was up early. It was cold, misty and raining. As the day wore on, the weather improved. Around midday, we broke camp and went through the usual process of corralling the draft reindeer, catching them and hitching them up to the sleds. Then Sergei led the way down the hill towards the north bank of the Seyakha River. Our group carried two small inflatable rubber dinghies, just big enough to bear two people. These were used to ferry everyone across the 100-yard-wide river.

The dinghies were also used to get the trains of reindeer sleds across. A rein from one of the front reindeer was attached to the boat, which a herder rowed across the river; the reindeer swam behind, pulling the sleds. The remaining draft reindeer were herded to the water's edge and they swam across too. It took a little over two and a half hours to get the 120 sleds and the 900 draft animals onto the far bank. The whole operation went remarkably smoothly and without any casualties. Sergei told me that the main herd was some 6 miles behind us and they would cross the following day. We made tea and ate raw reindeer meat on the river bank, before continuing the journey south. We travelled round a large lake and across an impressive marsh where the grass was knee-high, before finally making camp for the night only 500 yards from one of the drilling rigs.

Sergei was obviously eager to get away from Bovanenkovo as quickly as possible; so the next day, despite wind and rain, we moved again. We continued south, crossing the last of the raised roads. Now at least Bovanenkovo was behind us. After a few more hours of leisurely travel, I was surprised to see a tent in the distance. It turned out to be Sasha's uncle and aunt, whom I had first met in the spring. They were spending the summer by a lake with some of the young children.

We relaxed the following day, apart from the occasional excursion to collect firewood or to search for berries, as we awaited news of the main herd. In the evening, Sergei and some of the young men arrived and told us that the main herd had swum the Seyakha River without incident. They were making good progress and were now clear of the gasfield. Sergei and Sasha were obviously relieved.

A woman allows her reindeer to graze during a rest on the autumn migration.

The 600-mile journey to their winter pastures still lay ahead, but soon the first snow would arrive and they would be able to travel much more quickly. With luck, they would reach Yar-Sale by the middle of November, where about 25 per cent of the herd, mainly yearlings, would be slaughtered and sold by the state farm. The herders would then continue their journey south, taking the remainder of the animals to their winter lichen pastures in the forests south of the River Ob.

For Sergei and Sasha, the relief of leaving Bovanenkovo was tempered by the knowledge that when they returned the following year they would be faced by the same problems. It seems inevitable that in the coming years, as the gasfields are developed and more buildings, roads, pipelines and drilling rigs are built, the problems for the herders will increase.

It is the loss of grazing land that poses the biggest threat to the Nenet reindeer-herders. 'We have lost over one million hectares [2.5 million acres] of pastures to the gas industry in the last ten years,' Dmitrij Khorolya, the director of the Yarsalinskij State Farm, told me.

Whether reindeer herding can co-exist with gas development in the Yamal remains to be seen. It would certainly have to be on a much smaller scale. Many herders are deeply worried about the future. 'In 20 or 30 years' time, when all the gas is finished,' one of them said to me, 'Amoco and Gasprom will just go, but what kind of life will they leave behind for our children?'

A woman drives her reindeer sled past a gas-drilling rig at Bovanenkovo, Yamal.

In November 1992, Amoco had been instrumental in the setting-up of the Yamal Project Community Relations Group. Its membership is made up of gas company officials and representatives of native people's organizations, state farms, and local government. I was told that the group holds meetings with the Nenet reindeer-herders to 'discuss and address their particular concerns'.

I had the opportunity to see the Community Relations Group in action when I was invited to join them on a visit to one of the reindeer-herders' camps. A helicopter flew us from Yar-Sale to the 4th Brigade's camp out on the tundra. They, like Sergei and Sasha's group, had summer pastures at Bovanenkovo, and had already experienced some of the negative effects of gas development. The helicopter landed about 150 yards from the camp, and we trudged through the snow towards the tents. We were met by Hoodi Nudelit, the Group's leader, who invited us back to his tent. He showed traditional Nenet hospitality by offering us all a meal of reindeer meat, fish, bread and tea.

After we had eaten, the other herders and their families crammed into the tent, until it was bursting at the seams. In the dim light, a Gasprom official began the meeting by outlining the company's development plans for the gasfields. Everyone listened intently as he talked about the road and railway that would link Bovanenkovo to the south, and the pipeline that would transport the gas across Baidaratskaya Bay. He also spoke of compensation and of building houses, schools and power stations for the local people. The herders listened impassively – there is widespread mistrust of Gasprom officials by most Nenets.

Afterwards, Amoco's community affairs advisor briefly addressed the herders, assuring them that the Group had come to listen and help solve problems. A few of the younger men spoke out against gas development; others raised more immediate concerns, such as how to stop the workers' dogs at Bovanenkovo from killing their reindeer. Hoodi Nudelit never said a word throughout the meeting. It is doubtful that his silence was out of lack of interest or because he agreed with what he heard. More likely it was from fear of speaking out against authority, something that still lingers on in Russia from the old Communist days of the former Soviet Union.

To the older herders, Bovanenkovo had always been a summer haven – a dry place with plenty of fish, where the elders looked after the children while the younger men were out tending the reindeer. A father of ten, 62-year-old Hoodi Nudelit would probably have once been looking forward to spending summers at Bovanenkovo with his grandchildren. Now he was faced with the grim reality that there were drilling-rigs and buildings all over Bovanenkovo, and pollution and overfishing had virtually destroyed the fish stocks.

Although he must have realized that some of his guests represented organizations that threatened his family's livelihood, Hoodi Nudelit remained the perfect host, shaking hands and bidding them farewell. As the members of the Yamal Project Community Relations Group walked to the helicopter that would fly them back to their offices, they must have been totally unaware of the terrible tragedy that was about to unfold; for, later that night, Hoodi Nudelit hanged himself.

Acknowledgements

I am indebted to a great many people who helped me with my work on this book but I want to single out a few for special mention.

Firstly, my wife Cherry, who has been my toughest critic and most ardent supporter for the past 27 years.

It would have been impossible to produce this book if I hadn't received assignments from a number of magazine editors. These helped finance trips into the Arctic, and I am particularly grateful to Jonathan Fisher, John Nuhn and Steve Osmond for their support.

I want to thank my good friend Hans Jensen for all his help and kindness during my visits to Avanersuaq in Greenland.

Alexandre Bachkirov, Natasha Bogachova, Nikolai Garin, Kirill Gluschkoff, Valentina Golubchikova, Dmitrij Khorolya, and Sasha and Tanya Polyakov all proved invaluable during my work in Russia.

In Northern Quebec, I was helped by Abel and Elizabeth Brien, Thomas Coon, Brien Craik, Jimmy Rupert, and Susan Marshall.

In the Canadian Arctic, my thanks are due to George Qulaut, Mireille Matthieu and Bryan Robinson, Louis Tepardjuk, Leah Otak, Renee Wissink, Leah Williams and Kenn Harper; also to John and Carolyn MacDonald for all their help and hospitality over the years and for teaching me such essential Arctic survival skills as making caribou haggis.

Warren and Kari Hawkins helped keep me sane in the Norwegian Arctic during times of adversity.

Clive Stacey of Arctic Experience supplied air tickets to a number of northern destinations. So too did Max Johnson of the Great Canadian Travel Company. I am particularly grateful to Max and his wife Andrea for providing me with their own personal Medi-Vac service.

Edward Parker found time in his busy schedule to help edit the text.

Andrew Jackson of Advanced Colour Techniques made the outstanding quality duplicate transparencies from which the photographs in this book are reproduced.

Finally, I would like to thank all the native people of the Arctic and Sub-Arctic who shared their homes and food with me and allowed me the privilege of travelling with them and photographing their way of life in the forests and tundra of the North.

Bibliography

Arctic Wars – Animal Rights, Endangered Peoples, Finn Lynge, University Press of New England, 1992.

Contributions to Polar Eskimo Ethnography, Erik Holtved, C.A. Reitzels Forlag, Copenhagen, 1967.

Handbook of the North American Indians, Volume 5 – Arctic, Smithsonian Institution, Washington, 1984.

Handbook of the North American Indians, Volume 6 – Subarctic, Smithsonian Institution, Washington, 1981.

Intellectual Culture of the Iglulik Eskimos, Knud Rasmussen, Gyldendalske Boghandel, Nordisk Forlag, Copenhagen, 1929.

Lapp Life and Customs, O. Vorren and E. Manker, Oxford University Press, 1962.

Material Culture of the Iglulik Eskimos, Therkel Mathiassen, Gyldendalske Boghandel, Nordisk Forlag, Copenhagen, 1928.

Northwest Greenland – A History, Richard Vaughan, University of Maine Press, 1991.

Polar Peoples, Minority Rights Publications, London, 1994.

The Peoples of Siberia, M.G. Levin and L.P. Potapov, University of Chicago Press, 1964.

ABOVE *Jens Danielsen out in his boat hunting seals on a calm autumn day.*

Index

A grounded iceberg in North Greenland. The ridges are sculpted while the iceberg is afloat by air bubbles released as the iceberg melts. The bubbles travel up the side of the iceberg to the surface of the seawater, eventually cutting the ridges.